Into the Quick *of* Life

Jean Hatzfeld was born in Madagascar in 1949. A novelist and journalist, he worked for several years as foreign correspondent for the French daily newspaper *Liberation*, covering both the conflict in Yugoslavia and the Rwandan genocide. Since 2000, he has lived in Paris and Rwanda.

Jean Hatzfeld has recently received the Medici Prize for his latest book on Rwanda, *The Strategy of the Antelopes*.

Recommended by **pen**

This book has been selected to receive financial assistance from English PEN's Writers in Translation programme, in association with Bloomberg.

English PEN exists to:

- Promote literature and its understanding
- Uphold writers' freedoms around the world
- Campaign against the persecution and imprisonment of writers for stating their views
- Promote the friendly co-operation of writers and the free exchange of their ideas

Into the Quick *of* Life

*The Rwandan Genocide:
the Survivors Speak*

A Report by Jean Hatzfeld

Translated from the French by Gerry Feehily
Photographs by Raymond Depardon

This book was published with the help of the French Ministry in charge of Culture – The National Book Centre

First published as *Le Nu de la Vie* in 2000 by Editions du Seuil, Paris, France

First published in this edition in 2008 by Serpent's Tail

First published in this translation in the UK in 2005 by
Serpent's Tail,
an imprint of Profile Books Ltd
3A Exmouth House
Pine Street
London EC1R 0JH
website: www.serpentstail.com

ISBN 978 1 85242 989 8

Designed and typeset by Sue Lamble

Printed in the UK by CPI Bookmarque, Croydon, CR0 4TD

10 9 8 7 6 5 4 3 2 1

Contents

Introduction

I n 1994, about 50,000 Tutsis, out of a population of around 59,000, were massacred by machete, from Monday, 11th April at 11am to Saturday 14th May at 2pm, and thereafter every day of the week from 9.30am to 2pm, by Hutu militia and neighbours in the hills of the town land of Nyamata, in Rwanda. This is the book's starting point.

A few days earlier, in the evening of the 6th April, 1994, the plane bringing Juvénal Habyarimana, the President of the Rwandan Republic, back to Kigali, explodes above the airport. This attack triggers off the extermination of the Tutsi population, an extermination which, planned for months, begins at dawn in the capital's streets, and then spreads to the rest of the country.

In Nyamata, a small town in the hilly, marsh region of the Bugesera, the killings begin in the main street four days later. Crowds of Tutsis immediately seek refuge in churches or flee into the nearby banana groves, the marshes and the eucalyptus forests. On April 14th, 15th and 16th, in the churches of Nyamata, five thousand people are murdered – as many again in Ntarama, a hamlet twenty kilometres away – by militia, soldiers and by the vast majority of their Hutu neighbours. These two massacres inaugurate the genocide in this arid region of red clay laterite. It will last until mid May. For a whole month militias made up of disciplined, sober, singing killers, armed with machetes, spears and clubs, surround and pursue fugitives through the eucalyptus forest of Kayumba and the papyrus marshes of Nyamwiza. Their efficiency means that they kill five out of every six Tutsis, as many as in Rwanda's villages taken as a whole, far more than in the towns.

For several years, the survivors in the hills of Nyamata, as elsewhere, have remained silent, as enigmatic in their silence as the survivors of the Nazi concentration camps in the period immediately following their liberation. Some explain that for them, "Life broke in pieces", for others, "It stopped", and for yet more, "It absolutely has to begin again"; all admit, however, that amongst themselves the genocide is all they speak about. Which was the reason for coming back here to talk to them, to drink Primus beer at Marie-Louise's, or banana wine at the counter in Kibungo, to repeat the visits to these adobe houses, to sit at the terrasse of a *cabaret* – a bar – in the shade of acacia trees; to meet up, first shyly, then with greater confidence and familiarity, with Cassius, Francine, Angélique, Berthe and others, to persuade them to tell. Several of them proved sceptical as to the interest in speaking to a foreigner, as to the interest a foreigner might have in their stories, but none refused.

By way of explaining their long silence, they also say, for instance, that they "found themselves pushed to the side, as though they were in the way". Or, "they didn't trust humans", that they were too demoralised, outcast, "demolished". That they felt "embarrassed", or also sometimes "at fault" for having taken the place of an acquaintance, for having started again to behave like the living.

Farmers, shepherds, shopkeepers, teachers, a social worker, a mason's apprentice, they talked day after day, in Nyamata or in the surrounding heights, as indecision and reticence in summoning up certain memories dictated, and as new questions arose in the course of listening to them. Most of them, sceptical or indifferent as to the lessons history teaches, were, in spite of everything, glad to let another share in their present bafflement, their disarray and solitude.

*

A genocide is not an especially murderous or cruel war. It's a planned extermination. At the end of a war, survivors feel a strong need to bear witness; after a genocide, on the contrary, the survivors strangely long for silence. Such withdrawal is disturbing.

The story of the Rwandan genocide would be a long one to write. The purpose of this book, however, is not to add to the stack of inquiries, documents and sometimes excellent novels already published. It is solely to make available these astonishing stories of the survivors. A genocide, to use one of the survivors' own definitions, is an inhuman enterprise thought up by humans, too mad and too methodical to be understood. The stories Claudine, Odette, Jean Baptiste, Christine and their neighbours have told of their flight into the marshes; their narratives, often harshly and magnificently related, of their bivouacs, of their disintegration, their humiliation and their subsequent isolation; their apprehension as to the way others see them, their obsessions, the bonds that unite them, their doubts as to their memories; their experience as survivors, but also as Africans and villagers, bring us as close as we can get.

Background

The commune of Nyamata extends over fifteen hills with a total area of 398 square kilometres.

In March 1994, on the eve of the genocide, its population stood at approximately 119,000 inhabitants: approximately 60,000 Hutus and 59,000 Tutsis. Such a high ratio of Tutsis can be explained by the fact that the region, uninhabited during the first half of century, was first a land of asylum for large influxes of Tutsis at the beginning of the 1960s.

Around 50,000 Tutsis were murdered in the commune of Nyamata between the 11th April and 14th May 1994, the date of the arrival of RPF troops, meaning more than five out of six Tutsis. It's highly likely therefore, as Innocent Rwililiza explains, that if the killers hadn't been delayed by lootings and celebrations, they would have finished the job.

Around 22,000 Tutsis, repatriated from Burundi and Uganda in the main, came and settled the region from July, 1994 onwards.

Around 24,000 Hutus, on the other hand, have never returned from their exodus to the Congo.

Today, the population stands at 67,000 inhabitants, plus around 6,000 local prisoners native in the penitentiary at Rilima. The commune has registered 13,386 orphans.

Several hundred thousand Tutsis were murdered on Rwanda's territory in a twelve week period. Statistical research on the genocide is very difficult, because of the nature of the evidence.

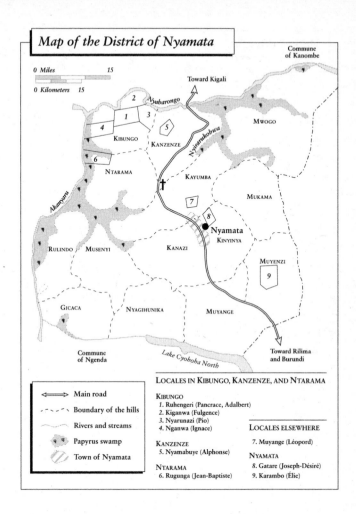

Map of the District of Nyamata

Commune of Kanombe

0 Miles 15

0 Kilometers 15

Toward Kigali

Nyabarongo

Commune of Kanombe

MWOGO

KIBUNGO

KANZENZE

Nyamwiga
Nyawankobwa

NTARAMA

KAYUMBA

MUKAMA

Akanyaru

Nyamata
KINYINYA

RULINDO   MUSENYI

KANAZI

MUYENZI

GICACA   NYAGIHUNIKA

MUYANGE

Commune of Ngenda

Lake Cyohoha North

Toward Rilima and Burundi

⟵⟹ Main road

- - - - Boundary of the hills

~~~~ Rivers and streams

Papyrus swamp

Town of Nyamata

LOCALES IN KIBUNGO, KANZENZE, AND NTARAMA

KIBUNGO
1. Ruhengeri (Pancrace, Adalbert)
2. Kiganwa (Fulgence)
3. Nyarunazi (Pio)
4. Nganwa (Ignace)

KANZENZE
5. Nyamabuye (Alphonse)

NTARAMA
6. Rugunga (Jean-Baptiste)

LOCALES ELSEWHERE
7. Muyange (Léopord)

NYAMATA
8. Gatare (Joseph-Désiré)
9. Karambo (Élie)

It will take several years therefore to make an accurate estimate of the number of victims of the Rwandan genocide, just as it took several decades to determine an exact figure for the victims of the Holocaust. Debates over the exact numbers are, right now, of no interest.

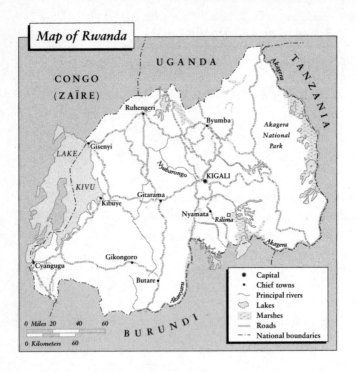

Map of Rwanda

Chronology of events in Rwanda and especially in Nyamata

1921 Under a League of Nations mandate, Rwanda and Burundi, formerly part of German East Africa and occupied by Belgian troops during World War I, fall under Belgian rule.

1931 Identity cards specifying the ethnic group of the bearer are introduced, a policy continued until 1994.

1946 Rwanda becomes a UN trust territory and is administered as a Belgian colony and part of Congo.

1959 The last great Tutsi king, Mutara Rudahigwa, dies. The Hutu peasant massacres and revolts that follow cause the exodus of hundreds of thousands of Tutsis.

1960 The Belgian Congo becomes independent, and Rwanda becomes a republic.

1961 The Hutu parties achieve victory in Rwanda's first legislative elections.

1962 The independence of Rwanda is proclaimed.

1963 In Nyamata, the Rwandan army carries out the first widespread massacres of Tutsis.

1973 Major Juvénal Habyarimana carries out a military *coup d'état*. Large numbers of Hutus fleeing poverty and drought flood into Nyamata, where renewed and repeated massacres occur.

1978 Juvénal Habyarimana is elected president.

1990 The Tutsi-led Rwandan Patriotic Front, which has been assembled from Tutsi militias operating out of Tanzania, Uganda, Burundi, and Zaire, gains its first military victories in Rwanda. Hutu extremist militias, called *interahamwe*, are organized by the Habyarimana clan.

1993 A peace agreement is signed in Arusha, Tanzania, between Habyarimana's regime and the RPF.

1994
April 6, 8pm. Habyarimana is assassinated when his plane is brought down by a mysterious missile on its approach to Kigali Airport.
April 7, early morning. Assassinations begin of political figures who did not fully support Habyarimana's dictatorship; the victims include Prime Minister Agathe Uwilingiyimana, a Hutu. RPF forces immediately begin their drive towards the capital, Kigali, where Hutu *interahamwe* militias have started slaughtering Tutsis and moderate Hutus. The genocide begins; it will continue for about a hundred days. In Nyamata, small-scale violence breaks out, definitively separating the two ethnic communities on the hills.
April 9. In Nyamata *interahamwe* troops launch the first raids to loot and burn houses abandoned by Tutsis and to murder rebellious Hutus; local farmers help them, but without receiving specific orders.
April 11. After waiting four days for directions from the government, Hutu soldiers from the base at Gako begin systematic killings in the streets of Nyamata. On the hills, the local authorities

and *interahamwe* assemble the farmers, and their planned attacks on Tutsis begin.

April 14–15. In Nyamata approximately five thousand Tutsi refugees are massacred by machete, first in the church, then in the Sainte-Marthe Maternity Hospital.

April 15. Some five thousand refugees are massacred in the church in Ntarama, thirty kilometres from Nyamata.

April 16. Organized hunts for Tutsis begin in the marshes of Nyamwiza and on the hill of Kayumba – wherever Tutsis have sought refuge.

May 12. Tens of thousands of Hutu families start fleeing towards Congo on the Gitarama road. The genocide in Nyamata is over.

May 14. The RPF reaches Nyamata and begins to look for survivors in the marshes.

July 4. Kigali centre falls to the RPF, which installs a new government with a Hutu president and General Paul Kagame as minister of defence. The RPF was eventually reorganized into the regular Rwandan army.

July 15. Half a million Hutu refugees begin to cross the border into Congo; eventually some 1.7 million Hutus fill the refugee camps of eastern Congo.

October 3. The United Nations Security Council endorses a report describing the massacres committed in Rwanda as genocide.

1996

November. Rebel forces opposing President Mobutu Sese Seko's regime invade eastern Congo, supported by Rwandan forces. Tens of thousands of Hutu refugees are killed, and some two million refugees eventually return to Rwanda. Most *interahamwe* either were killed during this Rwandan offensive or joined the return and gave themselves up to the Rwandan government, but some still live in Congo, in bands of looters or mercenaries, mostly in the Kivu region on the border.

1997

May 17. Troops of the Rwandan army sweep through Congo, driving out Mobutu and bringing Laurent-Désiré Kabila to power in Kinshasa.

1998

April 24. In Nyamata six condemned prisoners are publicly executed on the hill of Kayumba – to this day, the sole official executions there.

2002

January 1. The Third Republic is proclaimed in Rwanda, consolidating the regime of President Paul Kagame, who has been the strong man of the RPF from the start.

August. Gaçaça courts begin operating in Nyamata.

2003

January 1. A presidential decree is issued concerning those convicted of crimes of genocide. It authorizes the release of elderly and sick prisoners and allows probation – in conjunction with three days of communal labour per week – for convicts in the second and third categories (lower-echelon killers and their accomplices) whose confessions have been accepted and who have already served at least half their prison sentences.

1

Early morning in Nyamata

Grey cranes, with their trumpet song, are first to herald night's end in the Gatare quarter. Screeching touracos join in soon after, and the sun can hardly be far behind. In the morning mist appear flocks of storks and a swirl of pelicans gliding, hesitating, above the ponds. Then goats demand to leave the leafy pens built next to houses. The cows get the new day going; one by one, or in small herds, they vanish into the bush of Kayumba, spurred on by bare-chested boys wearing outsized jackets, with long sticks in the hand.

Up in the quarter's heights, the last alleyways, lined with mud dwellings, succeed one another to reach a patch of waste ground which turns into a football pitch, which marks the end of Nyamata's main street. This pitch, fitted out with cast iron goalposts, buckled in the dry season, covered in mud in the wet season, never stops groups of all ages from playing all day long. Lower down are the few brick houses where teachers, magistrates and shopkeepers live.

Here, Edith Uwanyiligira runs a guesthouse, made out of brick, in the shade of a small mango and papaya grove. The big yard out the back is overrun morning to evening by local kids, come in single file to fill water canisters from the only tap of running water in the area, between the kitchen hut and the domestics' shed. The children meet up in this yard at mealtimes, tempted by a huge pot which bubbles morning to evening, brimming with wheelbarrow loads of vegetables which the mistress of the premises brings back from market.

From the veranda you can hear, to the right, perched on branches, big beaked tomakos and lime green couroucous singing. Right opposite, you see clay and straw hovels, small gardens planted with beans, deep ditches where straw and dried mud building blocks are made; you see chickens, washing hanging off branches and draped over bushes.

A path, soon thronged with people on foot, on bicycle, a happy few on motorbikes, runs in front of the yellow district council building surrounded by a tall hedge in bloom. In the town hall courtyard local officials in white shirts talk with villagers come for an official stamp. In the car park, the magistrate's four-wheel drive van, the tractor which collects rubbish, single-cylinder motorbikes and bikes lean in clusters against the avocado trees.

It's in the town council that Innocent Rwililiza works, and a few hundred metres further on is Sylvie Umubyeyi's austere office.

Sylvie Umubyeyi is a social worker, and for this reason the first person I get to know in Nyamata. Having heard in Kigali that child survivors were roaming in small clans about the bush surrounding the region's marshes, I went to see her and to ask whether it would be possible to meet them. Sceptical or suspicious, Sylvie didn't want to help a foreigner make contact with these children so directly. On the road back to Kigali, however, we crossed paths at the entrance to the Memorial and had a short chat. This chance encounter seemed to change her mind. Straightaway, without explanation, she offered to take me in her van through the banana groves. She took me into the house of Jeanette Ayinkamiye, a teenage farmer, the abandoned children's chieftain, who we talked to one morning. Sylvie took me into the hills several times. At the same time she agreed to talk about herself, carefully at first, then freely and regularly. She is a captivating woman, and so arose the choice of the hills of Nyamata.

During a second visit, Sylvie asked Innocent Rwililiza to take up where she had left off. He proved to be just as attentive and understanding. Both of them became guides and friends, without whom these expeditions into the hills and these meetings with the survivors would have been impossible. On several occasions they also proved themselves interpreters of invaluable accuracy. It must be noted that these stories were related in three languages, firstly Kinyarwandan, the language of farmers, Rwandan French, spoken by other people and by translators, and finally French itself.*

On the way out of the village, the road turns left into the park in the grounds of the old parish church. This church is this little town's only piece of modern architecture. Today, its gaping walls and pockmarked roof bear the hallmarks of grenade explosions. Several times the Vatican Curia planned to restore the church and reopen it for religious services. But the inhabitants of Nyamata decided to keep it as it was and build there one of the region's two memorials; because it's here that the first massacre of a crowd of five thousand people took place, which itself led to the manhunt in the Bugesera.

In the church grounds, goats nibble on park shrubs. Their keeper is a twelve-year-old boy. He sits in the shade of a tree, a ball at his feet, a twig in his hand. His name is Cassius Niyonsaba. He is chatting with the Memorial's caretaker. He can be found every day of the week in the grounds near the church, which is half way between school and his aunt Thérèse's home. Sometimes he kicks the ball about with a friend; sometimes, like today, he is surrounded by goats; alone sometimes, he sits on a low wall behind the church looking at the vault. A deep scar, all along the crown of his head, parts his frizzy hair.

---

*In the translation, the translator has attempted to mirror these deviations from standard French.

Cassius Niyonsaba
12 years old, schoolboy
Ntarama hill

Papa was a junior teacher, Maman was a farmer. From my father's family, it is I alone who remained alive. From my mother's family, it is I alone, also, who remained alive. I can no longer remember how many big and little brothers and sisters I had, because my memory is all too preoccupied with this great number of dead, it is not nimble with figures anymore. This also slows me down at school.

But I can relive in all transparency the massacres at the church and the ferocity of the *interahamwe*. We call Hutu killers *interahamwe*. We got used to crossing their paths on the road. They hurled noisy threats at us. We could hear what they were saying, we said to ourselves that things were going badly, but reasonably we did not believe it. Later, after the plane accident, the neighbouring Hutus on my hill came every day to kill people where they lived, not even waiting for an everyday squabble or row. People then understood that things were serious, and they slipped away to the forest and the church. As for me, I went down to my big sister in Nyamata, which is why I did not die in Ntarama.

The day the killing began in Nyamata, in the street of the big market, we ran to the parish church. A large crowd had already assembled there, because when massacres begin it is Rwandan custom to take refuge in houses of God. Time granted us two peaceful days, then the soldiers and the local police came to patrol around the church, yelling that we would all soon be killed. I remember that you would think twice about breathing and speaking. The *interahamwe* arrived before midday, singing; they lobbed grenades, they tore down the railings, then they rushed into the church and started chopping people up with machetes and spears. They wore manioc leaves in their hair, they yelled with all their might, laughing scornfully from the throat. They thumped left, right and centre, they chopped randomly.

People who were not flowing in their own blood flowed in the blood of others, it was totally awful. Then they began to die without any more protesting. There was a great din and great silence at the same time. In the middle of the afternoon, the *interahamwe* burned little children before the front door. With my own eyes, I saw them writhing from the burns completely alive, truly. There was a strong smell of meat, and of petrol.

I no longer had any news of my big sister, I was all at sea. At the end of the afternoon, I got knocked on the head with a hammer, I fell, but I managed to slide away and hide with some boys behind a railing. When the *interahamwe* had finished working for the day, young people from our area, still brave enough to escape into the bush, carried me off on their backs.

The *interahamwe* finished off the killing in the church in two days; and immediately after they set off into the forest with machetes and clubs to track us down. With dogs in the lead, they searched to catch runaways hidden beneath cut branches. It was here that I was caught. I heard a shout, I saw a machete, I got a blow on the head and I fell into a hollow.

First, I ought to have been dead, then I insisted on going on living. I do not remember how. A woman passing that way, whose name was Mathilde, found me and carried me off to a hiding place under the *umunzenze*. *Umunzenze* are giant trees. Every evening, in the darkness, she brought me water and food. My head was going rotten, I felt as if the worms were gnawing near my brain. I thought that an evil spell had been cast upon me. But the woman laid African medicinal leaves on my head. This good-hearted woman was from Nyamata; I did not know her surname because I was from Ntarama, as I have already made known to you. She was Tutsi, the wife of a Hutu adminis- trator. When her husband found out that she had cared for a Tutsi child, he took her to the edge of the pond at Rwaki-Birizi, a good kilometre away – so it was reported to me later – and he killed her with a single thrust of his knife. Later, he joined the procession of those fleeing to the Congo, and no one has seen him since.

I can no longer properly remember the end of the genocide, because of the cut to my head. I had no more strength and hardly any more thoughts, the family home did not have a roof to it. I was laid very low by malaria, I had nothing but one pair of shorts. I had no one to go away with anymore, since everyone had been killed, in the church or in the marsh. So I returned to live in Nyamata at my aunt Thérèse's, who just works the land. I now live in the midst of her children, and other unaccompanied children like me. During conversations between children, it happens sometimes that someone speaks of the genocide, then each of us begins telling what we saw. This sometimes takes a long while. Sometimes, there is one of us who wants to change a detail here or there, but usually we repeat the same memories. Speaking together clears away pain.

I went back to school, to the fourth year of the primary. There are Hutu children on the benches, but I do not encounter any problems with them. Sometimes I play a little football, but it is usually the boys from Burundi who bring a ball along and put on soft shoes good for kicking around in. As for me, I like to chat with a friend, I also like to go on walks. I feel a little scrap of fear only when I go looking for firewood, far from the houses, because of the families who have come back from the Congo. When it is my turn to take care of my aunt's goats, I take them out to the bush in the company of those who look after cows.

But what I love most is to spend bits of time in the church courtyard. In the place where I escaped the massacres. Every day I go there, it is on the way to school. On Saturdays and during holidays I also go there. Sometimes I drive my aunt's goats, other times I take a friend who has a ball, or I sit alone. Every day I look at the holes in the walls. I go to the shelves,

I look at the skulls, the bones which were once all those people who were killed around me.

In the beginning, I felt a tendency to cry on seeing these skulls without names and without eyes looking at me. But little by little you get used to them. I stay sitting a long moment, and my thoughts go off in the company of all those before me. I force myself not to think of particular faces when I look at the skulls, because if I venture to think of someone I knew, fear catches up with me. I simply travel amongst all these dead who were scattered here and there and who were not buried. The sight and the smell of these bones causes me pain and, at the same time, soothes my thoughts though they trouble my head.

At school, we do not have time to talk seriously of all this. I also hear a great number of people urging me to abandon my memories, as bearers of evil. Which is the reason why I go back to the church. I like this peace here. After school I like to swap long sentences with the Memorial caretaker. His name is Epimaque Rwema. He tells me how Nyamata was a good town before the genocide, with many shops, a very solid football team, and cars in the street; how life seemed peaceful and was only difficult in times of drought. How people lost all control during the genocide; why neighbouring folk no longer wish to exchange words which could encourage pity. He explains to me why a number of people destroyed themselves despite deliverance. He also speaks to me about foreigners of good faith who now come to visit the bones at the Memorial, even about those who forget to leave little gifts.

I have heard that there were killings throughout the Bugesera and the rest of the country; but those at Nyamata were a little more bewildering because the evil-doers hacked women and children even to the cross. It is for this that the authorities gave us permission to build a memorial.

In the church, I clearly recognised one neighbouring man who was thumping. He was from Ntarama, and he thumped as though he could not stop himself. He was more than just out of breath. He was without a shirt on his back, the sweat oozed out of him everywhere, even though he was working his club in the shade of the roof. Often, near the market, I come across his family which has returned to its plot and that makes me feel uneasy. I know he is locked up in the prison at Rilima. I do not think he should live anymore; because a man who has thumped too much with his club has not a thought for those he has killed, and how he killed them, and he is never going to lose his appetite for killing. At the church I saw how ferocity can replace kindness in a man's heart, faster than a rainstorm. It is a terrible anxiety which unsettles me.

I believe that neither Whites nor even Blacks from neighbouring countries will ever totally believe what happened to us here. They will believe some bits of the truth and discount the rest. Even amongst ourselves, we are surprised when friends talk of killings in places where we were not, because the true truth about the killing of Tutsis is beyond each and every one of us. Which is the reason why, when I think about the people who chopped Papa and Maman and all my family, I wish they were shot, so as to drive my thoughts away from their sad fate.

I do not think that the *interahamwe* can offer one valid reason as to why they detest the Tutsis; they know only to repeat the same threats or accusations. It is said that they are afraid of something hidden in the Tutsis' nature, a peril which has disguised itself. The truth is that they covet Tutsi wealth too much, they are afraid there will be no more land for them one day, they are afraid of becoming their paupers. Even when Tutsis are poorer than they, Hutus want to burrow into their homes and take away the least little things. They have made their hearts go rotten on propaganda and greed.

When I am big, I will not go to mass anymore. I will never enter another church. I would like to be a teacher, because at school I benefit from the comfort of others, and because Papa was a teacher.

2

The big and little markets

A hundred metres away from the church Nyamata's main street emerges, lined with majestic *umuniyinya*, called "chit-chat trees". A wooden sign for an AIDS awareness campaign is the town's only bit of advertising. It marks the entrance to the market square, where boys, except during the scorching siesta hour, swirl around a football made from banana leaves.

Nyamata lives to the rhythm of two markets, the big and the little one. The big one takes place on Wednesdays and Saturdays, where at dawn, tradespeople lay their goods out on pieces of fabric spread on the ground. As is the case throughout Africa, the market is sectioned off in corporations. Here in one corner, fishermen's wives gather next to their fish, dried or smoked, strung together on creepers, protected from flies by the dust. In another corner are women farmers with mounds of sweet potatoes, bunches of bananas, sacks of red beans. Further on, shoes are piled up, in pairs or single, new or second hand. Stalls display luxurious cloths from Taiwan or the Congo snuggling next to piles of tee-shirts and underwear.

At the break of day, the crowd leaves little room for manoeuvre for the porters pushing long wooden barrows or for the women bearing wicker platters who keep the stalls stocked. Music is bought a little out of the way, in the street. The stall consists of a radio cassette player set on a stool for a trial listen, and three tables stocked with local music, traditional folk tunes from the Great Lakes, the melancholic songs of Annonciata Kamaliza, a famous Rwandan artist, and danceable hits from South Africa and the Congo. The music from the rest of the world is Céline Dion and Julio Iglesias.

The market is rather cheerful, modest, quite poor in fact, without jewellery stalls, without bric-a-brac traders, without anyone selling sculptures or paintings, without much in the way of bargaining or chit chat, without any flare-ups either.

As for the small market, it takes place every day on the bumpy waste ground behind the square. It's mainly a food market. Manioc is heaped up around the milling shed. The goat market is close by the slaughterhouse, in front of which stands a butcher's stall. Not far off are a veterinary pharmacy and clinic, and the *cabaret* – a bar – for local vets. Firewood sellers work hand in hand with charcoal merchants. You can also find cobblers remoulding flip flops, jerry cans of banana wine, jugs of buttermilk, turf and dried dung, heaps of trussed chickens, pyramids of sugar and salt, and everywhere, sacks of beans.

The market square is surrounded by shops painted in green, orange and blue, faded in the heat and dust. Half of them are shut and have been falling into ruins since the war. The other half house hairdressing salons and dark *cabarets* where men sip banana wine.

In Nyamata, there are no more newspaper stands or lay bookshops. For photocopies, you go to the parish bookshop. Near displays of coloured fabrics beneath shop awnings, close by the photo boutiques, seamstresses lean over wonderful black and gold Singer or Butterfly sewing machines. They stitch up torn trousers, make shirts to measure, sew hems on cloths, while their clients pay a visit to the church, to the chemist or to the local council.

Two days a week, Jeanette Ayinkamiye comes down from the hill of Kanazi to do some sewing at the market, in the midst of twenty sewing machines which clatter in the studious silence, interrupted occasionally by a burst of laughter, a snatch of advice. On these days, Jeanette wears her long Sunday dress with puffed out sleeves, but no jewellery, nor tresses, nor a fringe, all forbidden by her Pentecostal pastor.

The other days of the week, she works her family's plot. She dropped her studies after the genocide. She lives in an impeccably well-kept brick house with her two little sisters and two orphan children who she looks after, feeds, clothes and sends to school. She has never spoken to a foreigner before, but at the first meeting she agrees without hesitation to talk about herself. As the subject of her mother's death painfully and repeatedly comes up, she shows a remarkable determination to carry on.

Jeanette Ayinkamiye
17 years old, farmer and seamstress
Kinyinya (Maranyundo) hill

I was born among seven brothers and two sisters.
Papa was hacked the first day but we never found out where.
My brothers were killed shortly afterwards. With Maman and my little sisters we managed to escape into the marshes. For a month we endured beneath papyrus branches, hardly seeing nor hearing anything of the world anymore.

During the day, we lay in the mud in the company of snakes and mosquitoes, to protect ourselves from *interahamwe* attacks. At night, we roamed among abandoned houses looking for things to eat. Since we fed ourselves only on what we could find, we encountered many a case of diarrhoea; but fortunately it seemed that ordinary diseases, malaria and rain fever, wished to spare us this time round. We knew nothing of life anymore, except that all Tutsis were being massacred where they lived and we would shortly all have to die.

It was a habit with us to hide in small groups. One day, the *interahamwe* sprang Maman from beneath the papyrus. She stood up, and offered them money if they would but kill her with a single machete blow. They undressed her so as to take the money fastened to her cloth. They first chopped her two arms, and next her two legs. Maman murmured, "Saint Cécile, Saint Cécile", but she did not beg for mercy.

This thought makes me sad. But it makes me equally sad whether I recollect it by speaking aloud or silently to myself. This is why it does not embarrass me to tell you of it.

My two little sisters saw everything because they lay beside her, and they were struck too. Vanessa was wounded in the ankles. Marie-Claire in the head. The killers did not completely chop them up. Perhaps because they were in a hurry, perhaps they did so deliberately, as they had with Maman. As for me, all I could hear were noises and screams, because I was hiding in a hole a little further away. Once the *interahamwe* had gone, I got out and gave maman some water to taste.

The first evening, she could still speak. She said to me, "Jeanette, I leave without hope because I think you will soon be following me." She was suffering very much because of the cuts, but she kept repeating to us that we were all going to die and that this filled her with even more grief. I was not bold enough to spend the night with her. I first had to look after my little sisters, who were very hurt but not dying. The following day, it was not possible to stay with her, because we were forced to hide. This was the rule of the marshes: when someone had been badly chopped, you had to abandon them there for the lack of safety.

Maman lay in agony for three days before finally dying. On the second day, she could only whisper, "Goodbye, my children," and ask for water, but she still could not manage to go. I could not stay long with her because of the *interahamwe* attacks. I could see that it was all over for her. I understood also that for certain people, abandoned by all, for whom suffering had become their last companion, death must surely have been an all too long and pointless labour. On the third day, she could not swallow anymore, only moan softly and look about her. She never closed her eyes again. Her name was Agnès Nyirabuguzi. In Kinyarwandan, "Nyirabuguzi" means, "she who is fertile". Today, I often dream of her, a very precise scene in the middle of the marsh: I look at Maman's face, I listen to her words, I give her something to drink but the water does not flow down into her throat but spills straight from her lips; and then the attackers begin their pursuit again; I get up, I start running; when I return to the swamp, I ask people for news of my Maman, but no one knows her as my Maman any more; then I wake up.

On the last day of the genocide, when the liberators called to us from the edge of the marsh, there were some amongst us who refused to budge from under the papyrus, thinking that this was a new *interahamwe* trick. Later that evening, they gathered us together at the football pitch in Nyamata; the most able-bodied went off to root around in houses for decent clothes. Even though we could eat salted food at last, we had no cheerfulness to show, because we were thinking of the people we had left behind back there. We felt as we did in the marshes, except that no one was running after us anymore. We were not in danger of death anymore but we were still laid low by life. We looked for a home because my little sisters' wounds were infected. They stayed three weeks with the doctoresses before we could leave for our family plot. The house was destroyed. In the bush, we met Chantal Mukashema and her little cousin Jean-de-Dieu Murengerani, otherwise known as Walli. We gathered together in an uncle's house which had been looted, without a roof, without a bed, without even a scrap of fabric. Our life began again there.

Now we scratch the earth on our plot. We prepare food, laughing when we can, to bring the children closer to cheerfulness. But we no longer celebrate birthdays, because this pains us too much, and it costs too much money. We never row, not even once by chance, because we cannot find a how or a why.

Sometimes we sing school songs to one another. The two little girls have gone back to class. As for Jean-de-Dieu, he has been all too pensive since getting a machete blow on the head. He likes to stay seated, without counting the hours going by, his chin in his hand. One day, Chantal went off to marry a man whose name is François, but we still visit each other. As for me, I cannot contemplate marriage because of my little sisters and other obstacles. I encounter too much reluctance around me. In truth, I do not feel comfortable with life. I cannot think beyond the present.

Last year, our uncle's house was on its way to ruin. They moved us to Kanazi, to this solid house made from brick and corrugated metal, with a table, seats and pull-out beds. Here, my dark thoughts are not so dense. On Mondays, Tuesdays and Thursdays, I am a farmer on our plot or on those of neighbours who provide me with food and some pennies in exchange. On Wednesdays and Saturdays, I go to the market at Nyamata, and work on a Butterfly sewing machine. A girl, Angélique, has made room for me by her side. I sew on small patches for people who happen to come by, and I get by with this. I regret not being able to learn the sewing trade thoroughly, because then I could leave off labouring the land.

The children have emptied their minds of much misery, but they still have scars and headaches and thought-aches too. When they suffer too much, we take the time to return to those unhappy days. The two girls talk the most, because, concerning Maman, they saw it all. They often tell of the same scene and forget the rest.

Our memory alters over time. We forget the details, confuse the dates, mix up the attacks, make mistakes over names, and as to how such a man or woman or other acquaintance died, we are not in agreement. Nevertheless, we still remember all the terrible moments we personally lived through, as though they happened only last year. Over time, we still have very precise lists of memories; we talk to each other about them when we feel bad; they become more and more truthful, but we hardly know anymore how to order them in the right way.

When I find myself alone in the fields, I sometimes tend to look back on all this with too much grief. So I lay down my hoe and I go to see some neighbouring folks for a chat. We sing, share a juice together and this makes me feel well. On Sundays I go to church. I sing and I pray. I think that Satan chose the Hutus to accomplish all these horrors only because they were more numerous and stronger, and so they could spread more evil over a limited period of a few months. When I hear about these African wars on the radio, I am very worried. I think Satan is making the most of God's all too long absences from Africa to multiply all these massacres. I can only hope that the souls of all Africans who have endured all these misfortunes are given a proper reception.

The story of the Hutus and the Tutsis is like that of Cain and Abel, brothers who fall out over nothing at all. But I do not believe that the Tutsi people are like the Jewish people, even though both of them have been caught by a genocide. The Tutsis were never a people chosen to hear the voice of God, like the Hebrew people in pagan times. They are not a people punished for the death of Jesus Christ. The Tutsis are simply a people from the hills, unlucky because of their noble appearance.

In the marsh, Vanessa looked for a long moment into the eyes of Maman's killers. Two years later she recognised the face of one of these criminals, who was returning at his ease from the Congo, with his bundle. He was a boy from Kayumba, our pastor's eldest son. A boy who, in spite of everything, had had a long and good education. He sits it out now in the prison of Rilima, near Kidogo lake.

These prisoners are a torturous problem. If you imprison the hatred of these killers, then it can never dry out in the wide-open air. But if you let them slip back to the banana groves, the killings will begin again. I saw women throw themselves into the river, children in their arms, so their children's blood would not flow. Above all women, because women and children surely suffered greater torments than men. I am sure that if God does not catch the killers and give them a sermon himself, they will still want to start again. I place my trust in him because I would be all too anxious otherwise.

I think that once you have seen your mother being chopped with such wickedness, then suffering so slowly, you forever lose a part of your trust in others, and not only in the *interahamwe*. I mean that the person who has looked for such a long time on such a terrible suffering cannot live amongst people in the same way as before, because she will be on her guard. She will not trust them, even though they have done nothing to her. I mean to say that while Maman's death was the greatest sorrow for me, her all too long agony damaged me most, and this can never more be put to rights.

Also, I now know that a man can become of an incredible wickedness very suddenly. I do not believe that genocides have ended. I do not believe those who say that we have reached the depths of atrocity for the last time. When there has been one genocide, there can be another one, at any moment in the future, in any place, in Rwanda or elsewhere; if the cause is still there and we do not know what it is.

3

The Bugesera road

To get to the Bugesera from Kigali, you take a wide avenue, always jammed and uproarious, which zigzags down to the main road to Tanzania. After the last petrol station, overrun by long-distance taxi drivers, moneychangers, *awalé* players and cigarette girls, you leave the asphalt road and veer off south onto a pot-holed clay track. The track leaves the last outskirts behind, connects villages ever further apart; it goes past schools and churches perched on hillocks which shrink into the distance as the kilometres go by.

A grey yellow at first, little by little the track turns an ochre hue, then heads into landscapes coloured saffron, crimson, or purple, according to the sun's fancy. Far from the shimmering green of the tea hills of Cyangugu, and further again from the luxuriant green of Kibuye's tropical forests, the track snakes through a rolling landscape of clay and dusty scrubland. Fields planted with beans and sweet potato alternate with ragged banana groves; you pull up to let herds of easy-going cattle pass, guided by kids who reach no higher than their haunches; you overtake processions of women on foot, carrying bowls of manioc on their heads, babies slung on their backs. You come across the occasional van or minibus called "Dubai", whose suspension sags beneath an overload of passengers.

At the very end of a footbridge spanning the muddy waters of the Nyabarongo River, travellers, slumped on bundles of fabric, wait for a passing vehicle to give them a lift. As far as the eye can see, on either side of the footbridge, thousands of sacred ibises peck for food in the midst of black, round-tailed gangas and sultan water hens gliding in the reeds. Beyond this the Bugesera spreads out and the commune of Nyamata begins.

The district is defined by three marsh waterways. To the north and east, the Nyabarongo river, bound by the marsh of Butamwa; to the west the Akanyaru river, bound by the marsh of Nyamwiza; in the south, Lake Cyohoha and the marshes of Murago. These muddy valleys, covered in papyrus and giant water lilies, criss-cross the fifteen hills of Nyamata.

At the entrance to the commune, a piece of string stretched across the road announces a military checkpoint. The track then moves off into a red and green landscape. Ochre red from the laterite which clings to clothes, to skin, which covers floors; pale green from banana groves, papyrus, shrubs and scrub. In Kanzenze, the first village you come to, the houses are of mud brick with sheet metal roofs. Three *cabarets*, which to Rwanda are as *maquis* to the Ivory Coast and as *terrasses* to the Congo, opposite two warehouses, are the focal points of the area's public life.

On the right, a barely drivable road climbs up into an acacia forest, and leads up to the heights of Kibungo. Further on, a path heads down to the school at Cyugaro, which will be mentioned often in these stories as it served as a refuge; then it swoops further down to the Nyamwiza marshes which Jeanette has mentioned. In the trees, parakeets and jaco parrots with hooked beaks answer each other.

It's been ages since the village of Kibungo has seen a car. The deputy public prosecutor, the local councillor, the secretary of the local education authority all come here on their official motorbikes. The school headmaster, primary school teachers, a few shopkeepers and herdsmen ride bicycles, as often as not loaded with crates or jerry cans. Others, women coming back from market, teenagers coming out of secondary school, parish chorists, farmers gone to sell a goat or a sack full of produce, walk through the forest in an uninterrupted procession. At the last fork in the road, those on foot take a short cut up the dried up stone bed of a mountain stream, rejoining the cyclists at the first mud brick houses.

In the village square, a woman is sitting on a bench in front of her house, leaning back against the wall. Her name is Francine Niyitegeka. She smiles and introduces her baby, Bonfils, whom she cradles in her arms. Her niece, Clémentine, sits beside her. She wears a green cloth with a flower pattern, a matching fabric is wrapped around her head in a turban. You are struck by her beauty even from far off; close up, every gesture she makes is distinctive for its magical grace. She is getting ready to go to the district health centre, a twenty kilometre walk away, because her baby is suffering from a severe bout of malaria. The miraculous appearance of a car, an unexpected godsend on this torrid afternoon, encourages her to overcome her shyness. She laughs, and then, African-style, negotiates our first interview against a return journey in the car. The first day, she tells her stories in snatches, sparingly; she describes the tragedy in delicate ellipses. Her wariness dissipates in successive meetings. She is often talkative, sometimes cheerful.

Francine Niyitegeka
25 years old, shopkeeper and farmer
Kibungo hill

My parents were driven off their native land in the year of Independence, aboard a Belgian government truck, to come to clear a plot of land on the hill of Kibungo. Here, with the Hutus of the neighbourhood, we never truly mixed. Each lived in the midst of their own ethnic group, no one quarrelled. Our dealings were very much up and down, but there was a certain understanding nevertheless.

It was two or three months before the genocide began that

appalling incitements began to do the rounds from one plot to the next. Behind our backs, neighbouring Hutus yelled: "Tutsis, Tutsis, they must all die, absolutely!", and they hurled other similar threats. New faces began to appear among the houses, and we could hear the *interahamwe* shouting encouragement to one another as they trained in the forest.

The *interahamwe* began hunting down Tutsis on our hill on the 10th of April. The same day, we upped and left in a group, planning to stay in the church in Ntarama because they had never been known to kill families in churches. We waited five days. An endless flow of fellow farmers kept arriving, we came to be a large crowd. When the attack began, there was too much noise to take in every twist and turn of the killings. But I recognised many neighbours' faces as they killed with all their might. Very early on, I felt a blow. I collapsed between some benches, pandemonium all around. When I woke up, I checked to see that I was not dying. I crept out amongst the bodies and escaped into the bush. Amongst the trees, I came across a group of fugitives and we sprinted all the way to the marshes. I was to remain there a month.

Here we lived days darker than despair. Every morning, we hid the littlest ones beneath swamp papyrus, then we sat on the dry grass and tried to exchange calm words. When we heard the *interahamwe* arriving, we ran, splitting up in silence, deep into the leaves, and into the mud. In the evening, once the killers had finished their work and had turned for home, those who were not dead came out of the marsh. Those who were wounded just lay down on the damp riverbank, or in the forest. Those in one piece went to rest where it was dry, in the school at Cyugaro.

And very early in the morning, we went back down again, entered the marshland; we covered the weakest in leaves, to help them conceal themselves. In the marshes, we were confronted by the sight of many naked women, because when the Hutus killed they stole any decent cloths. Encounters such

as these truly made our eyes mist over with rage.

I found my fiancé Théophile again. We would catch sight of one another along the paths. We would linger a while together, but we lived without any intimacy. We felt too jarred to find the right words to exchange, to find tender gestures so as to touch one another. I mean that when we ran into each other it did not matter any more, neither for him nor for me; because, before anything else, each of us was thinking how to save ourselves.

One day, in my watery hiding place, I got caught. That morning, I had run off behind an old woman I knew. We were hunkered down in the water in silence. The killers sprang her first. They hacked her before my very eyes, without going to the trouble of pulling her out of the water. Then they meticulously searched the undergrowth because they knew all too well that a woman never hid alone, and they found me. I was holding my child in my arms. They slew it. I asked to be let up onto the grass and not die in the mire of mud and blood where the woman already lay. There were two men, of their faces I have not forgotten a single feature. They dragged me through the papyrus, and they laid me out with a blow full in the forehead, they did not chop my neck. Often, they left wounded people in the mud for a day or two, before coming back to finish them off. In my case, I believe they simply forgot to come back that way, which is why there is some work they left undone.

I lay in a dead faint for a long time: then Théophile and some other runaways found me there at death's door and restored me with water. I was only half alive. I was suffering from a bad fever and foul thoughts. I did not fear death anymore; nevertheless, the wounds chose to spare my head. I managed to get better without needing any more care. In the evenings, Théophile coddled me. He came with handfuls of food brought back from the fields. I finally brought myself back to life, I returned to the occupations of survival, I found my team again. In the marshes, we tried to stay with the same group of acquaintances, to make the task of comforting one other easier.

But if too many people died, we had to join a new team.

During the evening assemblies, we could catch hold of no news from anywhere because radio sets no longer blared out, except in the killers' homes. Still, we understood by word of mouth that the genocide had spread over the country, that all Tutsis were suffering the same fate, that no one would come to save us anymore. We thought that we would all have to die. As for me, I no longer concerned myself with thinking about when I would die, since we were going to die anyway, only with how the cuts would hack at me; only about how long it would take, because I was very frightened of the suffering machetes bestow.

I later heard that a small number of individuals had committed suicide. Especially women, who felt their strength withering away and who preferred the river currents to being chopped up. But to choose such a death demanded too great a folly, because the risk of being attacked by machetes grew on the path leading to the Nyabarongo.

The day of the liberation, when the RPF *inkotanyi* came down to the edge of the marshes, shouting to us that we could come out, no one wanted to move from under the papyrus. The *inkotanyi* yelled their lungs out with words of reassurance, while we stayed beneath the leaves, without uttering a word. I think that at this moment we, the survivors, mistrusted every single human being on earth.

As for the *inkotanyi*, when they saw us coming out at last, like mud vagabonds, they looked put out. Above all they looked amazed; as though they were wondering whether we were still human beings, after all that time in the marshes. They were more than embarrassed by how scrawny and stinking we were. Despite the disgust in the situation, they wished to show us great respect. Some chose to stand stiffly to attention in their uniforms, lined up in rows, their gazes fixed upon us. Others decided to come close to support the most badly off. You could see that they had trouble believing it all. They wanted to show themselves as very kind, but they hardly dared utter a word to us, as if we were no longer able to understand anything. Except, of course, soothing words of encouragement.

Four months after the genocide I married Théophile. We acted as though nothing had changed between us, despite what had happened. In this way we came back to each other again, saying quietly what needed to be said quietly, saying aloud what could be said aloud. We live in a three-room clay-brick house with a sheet metal roof with our two little children and four orphans. As for the orphans, there is no more point in talking to them of the genocide; they have seen reality at its worst. My two little children will later learn the necessary truth about the genocide. That said, I think that a gulf of understanding now separates those who lay down in the marsh and those who did not; between you and me for instance.

With neighbours, we talk of the killings nearly every day, otherwise we dream of them at night. Talking does not soothe our hearts, because with words we cannot return to times past. But to be silent encourages fear, withdrawal, and all such feelings of mistrust. Sometimes we joke about it all, we laugh, yet still we come back in the end to those fatal moments.

I do not want to weep vengeance, but I hope that justice will offer us our share of peace of mind. What the Hutus did was unbelievable, above all for us, their neighbours. The Hutus have always imagined the Tutsis are haughtier, more civilised than they, but this is rubbish. Tutsis react more soberly in misfortune and in happiness. They are simply more reserved in their behaviour. It is also true to say that Tutsis are better at preparing for the future – it is in their tradition. In the Bugesera, in any case, no Tutsi ever visited any harm on a Hutu; they never had an offhand word to say for them on their account. They were just as poor on the hillsides, their plots were no bigger, and they had neither more health nor education than the Hutus.

I do not know whether there is any great point or not in talking about all this now. I do it with doubts because so many people here are no longer able to speak on their own account, while fate has granted me the opportunity to speak on mine.

Hutus still suffer from misconceptions about the Tutsis. It is our appearance which is at the origin of this evil – that is the truth. Our muscles are longer, our features more refined, our gait is stiffer. The proud bearing we were born with, that is all I can see.

What the Hutus did is more than wickedness, more than punishment, more than barbarity. I cannot say anything more precise than this; because even if an extermination can be shared in conversation, it cannot be explained in an acceptable way, even amongst those who lived through it. A new question we had not foreseen always crops up.

My family is dead, and as for me, due to my headaches, I cannot work the soil in the sun anymore. I do not know why God chose that I should not die, since I was ready to expire, and I thank Him. But I think of all those who were killed, of all those who killed. I say to myself, I did not believe the first genocide would happen, so as to the chances of a second one, I cannot really answer. Frankly, I believe that the suppression of Tutsis is over for our generation; after that, no one can predict our future. I know that many are the Hutus who criticised the massacres, saying that they felt obliged to join in. I see Hutus lowering their eyes for the great guilt they feel. But I cannot glimpse much goodness in the hearts of those now returning to the hills, and I hear no one asking for forgiveness. In any case, I know there is nothing to forgive.

Sometimes, when I am sitting alone, in a chair, on the veranda, I imagine this possibility: one day, in the distant future, a neighbour will walk slowly up to me and say, "Good morning, Francine. Good morning to your family. I have come to speak to you. Alright, it is I who hacked your Maman and your little sisters, or it is I who tried to kill you in the marsh. I want to ask your forgiveness." Well, to this person, I would not have a good word to answer with. If a man has drink one

Primus too many and he beats his wife, he can ask for forgiveness. But if he has worked a whole month killing, even on Sundays, how can he hope for pardon?

We simply have to get back to living again, since life has decided it so. Thorn-bushes must not overrun our plots; teachers must be in front of the blackboards at school again, doctors must again treat the sick at the health centres. We need young cattle in fine fettle, fabric of all qualities, sacks of beans at the market. Many Hutus are needed for all this. We cannot lump all the killers together. Those who were carried away by it in spite of themselves can come back from the Congo and from prison and go back to their plots. We will start drawing water together again, exchange some local gossip, sell each other grain. In twenty, fifty years time, perhaps there will young boys and young girls who will learn of the genocide from books only. For us, though, it is impossible to forgive.

When you have lived through a waking nightmare for real, you can no longer sort your day thoughts from your night ones as before. Ever since the genocide, I have felt pursued day and night. In bed, I turn away from the shadows; on the road, I look back at the figures that follow me. I am afraid for my child each time my eyes meet those of a stranger's. Sometimes, I see the face of an *interahamwe* near the river and I say to myself, "There you are, Francine, you have already seen this man in a dream," only to remember later that the dream was my time, wide awake, in the marshes.

I do not think this will ever be over for me, to be so despised for having Tutsi blood. I think of my parents who had always felt hunted in Ruhengeri. I feel a sort of shame to have to spend a lifetime feeling hunted, simply for being what I am. The very moment my eyelids close shut on all this, I weep inside, out of grief and humiliation.

4

Kibungo hill

In Kibungo, Francine, wife of first local councillor, Théophile Mpilimba, runs the village *cabaret* bar, so modest that it doesn't have a sign, in a small house adjoining her own. The walls are of clay and straw, the ground is beaten clay, the window tiny. Crates of Primus beer vie for space at the back with sacks of potatoes or beans and bottles of oil. Benches on which clients sit when it rains run along the walls. Stools are there by the door for them in good weather. The usual drinks are *urwagwa*, a strong and bitter banana wine, or *ikigage*, a sorghum wine – not as "tasty" – containers of which are lined up behind the counter.

Banana wine is made without a still according to an ancestral recipe. Bananas are buried in a ditch for three days to get them over-ripe, then the juice is squeezed out, mixed with sorghum flour, which triggers fermentation, and is left to alcoholize for four days to become a drink somewhere between sweet wine and marc. It absolutely has to be drunk within the week that follows, before it inevitably turns sour. Once, Kibungo's *urwagwa* was the region's most famous. Once, the hill of Kibungo, with its silt-laden land along the river, used to be the most fertile.

Before the genocide, the hill was divided, Tutsi houses running down one side of the hill, with herds of cattle all the way down to the valley; and on the other slope Hutus, producing most of the alcohol and bean crop. Today, the land is bereft of two thirds of its men, and alcohol often runs out at Francine's.

Cattle are thinly scattered here and there amidst the shrubs.

The village spreads out across a flat on the top of the hill. At the entrance, brick buildings – a little church, schools, the town hall – surround majestic *umuniyinya* trees, in the shade of which people are called to sit during public assemblies or civic announcements. About the village, other *umuniyinya* are most likely to be frequented by sleepers lying around.

Among the houses on the summit, a swarm of kids playing football vie with the goats for their grazing area, kicking a ball made out of mattress foam made tight with bits of string. No dogs loll about the gardens, all of them having died, or having run off in packs since the war, and there are few chickens, prey to wild cats. On the way out of the village, the path leads down to the river, comes across cattle pens made from tree trunks tied up with creepers, rubs up against Hutu hamlets whose inhabitants, kids excepted, no longer venture into the village, except to sell their *urwagwa*.

Denise, an eighteen-year-old Hutu woman, lives in a house near the river with her sister Jacqueline, two little brothers and sisters and her baby. Her parents and her four big brothers haven't returned from their exile in the Congo. Denise shows herself to be very hospitable and considerate. She talks about her happy adolescence on the hill, the choir, school parties, boys. She mentions her melancholic existence today, how, having despaired of ever finding a real husband, she is now "second violin" for a wealthier farmer, father to her child, who lives two hundred metres further down. She sends the children to the local school without accompanying them, walks through the forest every week to the market at Nyamata to sell fish.

From her veranda, you admire a panorama of treetops and, in the valley, the green expanse of the marsh of Nyamwiza, a place of refuge mentioned by Jeanette and Francine. Despite its obvious proximity, she claims not to have heard or seen anything during the massacres, no longer knows where her family was in

April, 1994, has had no news of their exile. At the mention of the word genocide, she walls herself up in silence. All her Hutu women neighbours react in the same way.

Beyond her field planted with manioc, the trail swoops down and ends at Akonakamashyoza, an islet of mythical reeds where the rivers Nyabarongo and the Akanyaru meet, on which narrow dugout canoes glide by. It's here, the fishermen claim, that during the reign of Tutsi kings, the day after one of them had died, that at the confluence of these two sacred tributaries of the White Nile, the procession of the Living King, the heir, would pass, in the light of the sun; followed by the procession of the Mummy, the dead king, by moonlight.

In the middle of the Kibungo afternoon, when everyone has returned from the fields, woman settle down in their gardens, shelling beans and keeping an eye on kids and pots. Men stride purposefully off to the *cabaret*. At Francine's, you don't often hear someone ordering a beer, because beer is expensive. The most well off men buy a bottle of *urwagwa*, into which Francine pops a reed stem. They drink and pass the bottle round, at the same time as they pass cigarettes round. The poor can only afford drinks by the mouthful, with the help of a longer straw stuck in a jerry can behind the counter, under Francine's benevolent gaze.

Later, as daylight fades, you hear cattle bellowing. Returning cowherds join the drinkers; amongst them, Janvier Munyaneza, a young boy. Janvier looks after his big brother's cows, and those of a neighbour's, which stops him from going back to school. Once he has rounded up the cows in their pen, and cleaned the tics off them, it's his turn to come sit at the counter. He doesn't drink alcohol yet and with a greedy smile accepts the offer of a sweet Fanta. His shyness is typically Rwandan. Sitting in the middle of a group of children and adolescents, he watches the adults drinking and telling stories until late in the night. His eyes reflect a melancholy which the taciturn voice of first words confirm.

Janvier Munyaneza
14 years old, cowherd
Hill of Kiganna (Kibungo)

At school, I never heard an ethnic reproach. We kicked a football about together without any hassles between us, when time grudged us a bit of permission, that is. On the 10th of April, after mass, neighbouring Hutus came to our house near the river and ordered us to clear off because they wanted to seize it, without killing us though. We immediately went up to Kibungo, to live with my grandfather.

The next day, the soldiers arrived; my uncle tried to slip away; they shot him dead near the door. So we then fled towards the church in Ntarama, Papa, Maman, my eight brothers and sisters, my grandfather and grandmother. The *interahamwe* prowled about the small wood around the church for three or four days. One morning, they all came in a group together, behind soldiers and local policemen. They broke into a run and started hacking people, inside and outside. Those who were massacred died without saying a word. All you could hear was the commotion of the attacks, we were almost paralysed, in the midst of machetes and the assailants' cries. We were almost dead before the fatal blow.

My first sister asked a Hutu of acquaintance to kill her without any suffering. He said yes, and he dragged her by the arm out onto the grass, where he struck her with a single blow of his club. But a next door neighbour, nicknamed Hakizma, yelled that she was pregnant. So he ripped open her belly like a pouch in one slicing movement with his knife. This is what these eyes saw without mistake.

I crept out among the corpses. Unfortunately, a boy managed to push me with his metal bar, I dropped onto the bodies, I didn't move anymore, I made dead man's eyes. At one moment, I felt myself being lifted and thrown, and other people

fell on top of me. When I heard the *interahamwe* leaders whistle
the order to pull out, I was completely covered in dead people.

It was towards evening that some courageous Tutsis from
the area, who had scattered into the bush, came back to the
church. Papa and my big brother pulled us free from the heap,
me and my very bloodied youngest sister, who died a little later
in Cyugaro. In the school, people put dressings of medicinal
herbs on the wounded. In the morning, the decision was made
to take refuge in the marsh. This was to happen again every day,
for a month.

We went down very early. The little ones hid first, the
grown-ups acted as look-outs and talked about the disaster that
had befallen us. When the Hutus came, they were the last to
hide. Then there was killing all day long. In the beginning, the
Hutus played tricks in the papyrus, for example they said, "I've
recognised you, you can come out" and the most innocent got
up and were massacred standing. Or else the Hutus were
guided by the cries of little children, who could not stand the
mud anymore.

When they found rich people, they took them away so they
would show them where their money was hidden. Sometimes
the killers waited until they had caught a big group, to hack
them all together. Or until they had rounded up a whole family,
then cut them one before the other, and this left a great expanse
of blood in the marsh. Those who were still alive went to
identify those who had been unlucky, looking at the bodies
lying in puddles.

In the evening, in Cyugaro, people grouped together:
neighbouring folk amongst themselves, the young with the
young... In the beginning, little groups assembled to pray. Even
people who had never had a long-standing habit of praying
before – somehow it seemed to soothe them to believe in a
small invisible something. Later though, they lost strength, or
faith, or they simply forgot, and no one minded about that
anymore.

The old liked to meet together off by themselves, to discuss what was happening. There were young people who brought them small but sufficient quantities of food. But certain old people had no longer any more children to help them. Every evening, they could feel a decline growing upon them, because they had not enough strength left to dig the earth and take care of themselves. Given their great age, they had too much self-respect to go begging. So one evening they would say, "Alright, I'm good for nothing anymore, tomorrow in the marsh I shall not move." This is how many of them let themselves perish, sitting early in the morning against a tree, no longer fighting to the very end.

On certain evenings, when the evil-doers had not killed too much that day, we gathered around glowing embers to eat something cooked; on other evenings, we were too dispirited. In the marsh, at dawn the next day, we found the same blood in the mud. Corpses going off in the same places. The evil-doers preferred to kill as many as possible without taking the trouble to bury them; they must have thought that they would have time later, or that they would not be made to do this stinking chore since they had already done enough. They also thought that the sight of these dirtied corpses in the mud would put us off from hiding. As for us, we did try to bury a few of our relations' corpses, but there was rarely time. Even those animals who would have eaten them had all fled because of the din of the killings.

These corpses offended our spirits to such an extent that, even amongst ourselves, we did not dare speak of them. They all too bluntly showed us how our own life would end. I am trying to say that their rotting made our death more barbarous. Which is the reason why our utmost wish in the morning was simply to make it through to the end of the afternoon one more time.

When the *inkotanyi* came down to the marsh, to tell us that the massacres were over, that we were to remain alive, we did

not want to believe them. Even the weakest refused to come out from the papyrus. The *inkotanyi* turned back without a word. They returned with a boy from Ntarama. He started shouting: "It's the truth. They're *inkotanyi*, they're RPF. The *interahamwe* have run off in disarray. Come out, you won't be killed anymore." We got up. It was the first time in a month any of us had seen each other standing up in the middle of the afternoon. At the assembly, a soldier explained to us in Swahili: "Now you are saved, you must leave your machetes and knives here. You shall not need them anymore." One of us answered: "We have not had any machetes since the beginning. We have only diseases on us but those we cannot drop here. We do not even have clothes any more." I was wearing just a pair of ripped shorts, the same shorts since the first day.

We left the worst off in the shade, to pick them up later aboard some vehicles. We were escorted to Nyamata, we waited a few days, then with my big brother we went back to our plot in Kiganna. Since the family home had collapsed, we settled here, in Kibungo, in the house of the grandfather who during this time had been killed. In any case, it was all too heavy a burden to live by the edge of the river where we had been happy as a family.

Papa had twenty-four cows and five goats. We were able to catch three of them in the bush, thanks to their very distinctive mottling. I now live with my big brother, Vincent Yambabaliye. I prepare a bowl of food for him morning and evening, I look after our cows in the shrubbery and three other ones belonging to neighbouring folk, while he cultivates the plot. I do not like going down into the valley, because I am afraid the cows will go off with herds belonging to shopkeepers of Nyamata. We do not have enough cows to have them looked after by a paid cowherd. This is what stops me from going back to school, and this is a strong daily sorrow.

In Kibungo, I brought myself back to life not too badly, but the grief over having lost my family always keeps turning up unexpectedly. The life I lead is all too desolate. Out in the cattle's company, I fear rustlings in the coppice. I would like to go back to the benches and begin a school life again, where I would be able to glimpse a future for myself.

In Kibungo, I can see all too well how broken life is the moment evening comes. Many men are waiting impatiently to drink *urwagwa* or Primus. *Urwagwa* is our banana wine. They drink and can no longer think anything interesting, they babble absurdities, or they are completely silent. As if they only wished to drink in the place of all those who were killed and who cannot drink their share with them anymore, and, above all, no one wants to forget.

We will never forget a single scrap of truth about the genocide in Kibungo, because we share our memories. We often talk about this in the evenings, we go over the details with one another, we seek clarifications. Some days, we evoke the most terrible moments, the threatening *interahamwe*; on certain days, we evoke the quieter moments, when they had a day off on our side of the marsh. We let fly funny jibes at each other, then the next minute we are back to the most painful scenes.

That said, because of time, I can feel that my memory is sorting out my memories as it pleases, without my being able to affect this; the same for my companions. There are certain episodes which are very often retold, so they grow thanks to all the additions one person or another brings to them. Their transparency is maintained, if I can put it so, as if they happened yesterday or no more than last year. Other episodes are left behind and they grow obscure as in a dream. I would say that certain memories have been perfected, while others are neglected. But I know that we remember better now than we used to the things that happened to us ourselves. We are not interested in making things up anymore, in exaggerating, or hiding things as we did at the liberation, because we are not muddled by the fear of machetes anymore. Many people are less frightened or less embarrassed of what they lived through.

Sometimes, we talk about ourselves too much, and I take fear when I lie down in my bed.

When I walk by the church at Ntarama, I turn my eyes away all along the railings, I avoid the hut of the Memorial. I do not want to look at rows of nameless skulls which are perhaps those of my family. Sometimes, I go to the edge of the marsh, sit down on a tuft of grass and watch the papyrus. Then I see the *interahamwe* again, hacking with machetes at what they have found during the day. Inside me, then, feelings of sadness and menace, but not of hatred.

To feel hate, you would have to be able to point it at particular faces or names; for instance, those you recognised as killers, you would have to curse them in person. But in the marshes, the killers worked in columns, and from beneath our leaves we hardly ever made out their features. Anyway, as for me, I cannot manage to call a single recognisable face to mind anymore. Even my sister's killer's face I have forgotten. I think that if hatred dissolves when faced with a crowd of strangers, it is the opposite for fear. In some ways, this is what I feel.

If I try to come up with an answer for these massacres, when I try to know why we had to be hacked, my mind comes in for a rough ride; and I am no longer sure about anything around me. I will never be able to grasp our Hutu neighbours' way of thinking. Even those neighbours who did not actually hack, but did not say anything. These people wanted to speed up our death to grab hold of everything. I can only see greed and power as the roots of this evil.

I do not understand why as an ethnic group we are cursed. If it were not for the obstacle of poverty blocking my way, I would travel far away from here. To a country where I would go to school all week, where I would play football in a cultivated meadow and where no one would mind to be mistrustful and kill me.

5

Horns the shape of a lyre

In the Bugesera, photographing a cow without having a serious palaver with its owner or a gift for its herdsman is unthinkable. Nevertheless, cows are omnipresent – in the undergrowth, in the forests, on playing fields and school lawns, amongst gardens and vegetable patches, in the middle of the street. But in Rwanda a cow is much more than just livestock. "The cow is the supreme gift," goes one of the innumerable sayings.

A cow is a sentimental offering, a gesture of friendship; or it's a loan, a reward, a bribe, a dowry, an investment several families make to provide milk for the children. Two cows make a herd. Beyond that, you can never say the number aloud, because this brings bad luck. Often cattlemen group five, twenty, thirty beasts together and put them out to one ragged herdsman, so as to protect them from envious looks.

The Rwandan cow is of the ankolé breed, the name of the region in Uganda where it settled for a long time. The breed is said to have come down from Upper Tibet, to have crossed Persia, then Abyssinia, after which it fanned out towards the region of Great Lakes, then Senegal and South Africa. European historians date its entry in Rwanda back to the end of the twelfth century. Tribes of Hamite nomads, the Tutsi's ancestors, drove gigantic herds into the hills and valleys and settled the summit, from where they had control over the Hutus living in the fields below and the Twa pygmies in the forests. This theory was taken up again by the genocide's theorists trying to legitimise a Tutsi extermination and the destruction of their herds. Ideology aside, however, this theory is contested by more and more African and European historians. Cave paintings in several prehistoric sites in the Great Lakes region (contemporaneous with the cave paintings of the Mesopotamian epoch) attest to an earlier culture of cattle and cattle-breeders from the great Bantu and Sudanese migrations at the beginning of the Christian era.

The ankolé is of a thin, muscular, medium build. A slight cervical hump makes it look like the zebu. Its hide is most often an even tawny colour, or a mottled grey or black or brown and white. It's remarkable for its splendid, lyre-shaped horns, both powerful and tapered. For centuries, in fact, the sole criterion in selecting and crossbreeding an animal has been the beauty of its horns. To the great displeasure of vets, who have tried without success to promote crossbreeding with European strains and high calorie feeding methods.

Half-tame, half-wild, the ankolé is neither a good dairy nor meat animal. Indeed, beef is rarely eaten in the Bugesera, and when the occasion arises, it's one to be regretted – so tough and stringy is the meat, unlike the delicious goat meat kebabs grilled on street corners. Rwandan cattle breeders balk at slaughtering or meddling with the purity of the breed. "A single cow puts you under as many obligations as a herd, and more than a daughter," goes another saying. Breeders like to show them off, give them away, and above all make their number increase.

Farmers at heart, Hutus consider cattle rearing an unjustifi-able luxury in an overpopulated country of arid slopes. They disdain cattle even more so given that, before the Republic, they symbolised all the power of the Tutsi kings, who did not hesitate, during festivities, to parade for days on end vast herds of cattle, horns embellished with grease, like others parade their armies.

This is why, as of the first days of the genocide in the Bugesera, the *interahamwe* slaughtered their victims' cattle. To eat them, to abolish them. Today, many Hutus reveal scenes where the murderers cut the animals' throats before their owners' eyes first, to humiliate them, and before killing the owners themselves. Accounts are also sprinkled with allusions to gargantuan barbecues on the evenings following large-scale massacres. In the Bugesera, and throughout the Rwandan territory, two thirds of the national livestock was destroyed during the killings, but it has since been replenished. The energy the survivors displayed in finding stray cattle, in bringing new cattle in from Burundi and Uganda, in calving them, in putting them out up in the deserted heights, in offering them to friends all too bereft by the extermination of their families, illustrates the vitality of the tradition.

Many well-intentioned ethnologists, Rwandan expatriates and journalists play down the distinctive differences between the Hutu and Tutsi ethnicities. But country people love nothing better than resembling the stereotypes strangers have of them. This is also true of the Argentinian gaucho, the Provençal fishmonger, or Tahitian women; the Tutsi cattle-farmer is no exception to the rule. You will never see a Hutu farmer walking along holding a long stick, a felt hat on his head; but you will often see his Tutsi counterpart wearing those cattle-breeders' accessories and, in the evening or at the weekend, you shouldn't be too surprised to see this or that school principal, bureau chief, this or that shopkeeper or doctor walking into the café holding his staff, sporting a hat – signs that he owns a cow in a herd.

Jean-Baptiste Munyankore, a very dignified man of sixty years, teacher at the school of Cyugaro for twenty-seven of them, is attached to this custom. He wears a white short-sleeved shirt in the classroom through which he gives you a tour, walking between rows of impeccably smooth wooden desks, stroking them with all the pride of a winemaker amongst his casks. He dons a jacket and a tie before going to staff meetings, but for the local *cabaret* and when going into town on a Saturday, he always takes his long cattle-breeder's staff. Jean-Baptiste inspires all the respect due to an elder, because he was part of the first wave of pioneers who fled the massacres at the end of the reign of the Tutsi kings.

Jean-Baptiste Munyankore
60 years old, teacher
Hill of Cyugaro (Ntarama)

I was a young man when we were exiled to the Bugesera. This was in 1959, the *mwami* Mutara III had surrendered his last breath, all positions of importance were in Hutu hands after Rwanda's first popular elections. I had finished my studies in the famous Teacher's School of Zaza. I was given a post in the volcanic region of Birunga, but the moment I tried to set foot in the classroom, I was pushed back out, and I could hear more and more worrisome words pronounced behind my back.

In December of that awful year, Bahutu extremists painted the doors of Batutsi houses with a single brush stroke during the day, then came back during the night to torch them. So we took refuge along with a company of neighbours at the Catholic mission, where no one at that time would dare come to push us about. Day after day, we came to be too numerous and began pushing one another aside. The Belgians tried hard to save us but above all they feared all the squalor. So one morning a Belgian administrator came; he asked us to write down on a list the country to which we wished to be exiled. I knew nothing good of foreign countries, I had family neither in Burundi nor in Tanzania, so I wrote down the name of Rwanda, my own country. A large group of us had written down the same answer. The administrator concluded by saying: "Alright, you will go to the Bugesera, since it is uninhabited."

We only knew the Bugesera region by name. They brought army trucks into the mission yard. I got aboard a *rubaho*, a truck with a wooden skip, with my wife, my little brother and my grandmother. We were only allowed to leave with the shirts on our backs and nothing else; neither utensils, nor blankets, nor books. This is how we travelled for a night, without stopping, not knowing what lay in store for us. Not once on the road did I cast a backward glance and I never set foot again in the commune of my childhood. We crossed the bridge over the Nyabarongo river early in the morning. At the time, it was only two tree trunks placed in the water to get you over. On the other side, other lorries were waiting for us.

We opened our eyes to a land of savannah and marsh, we were arriving in the Bugesera. I thought to myself : "They are packing us in here, abandoning us alive into the arms of death." I am not exaggerating when I say the tsetse flies darkened the clarity of the sky. To this day, I still believe the authorities presumed that these terrible tsetse would be the end of us. We could not see a single living being anywhere on the trail, then the first straw huts appeared. As for wood lodgings in Nyamata, there was but the mission office, the district court, the administrator's home, and an army camp in the forest of Gako.

After a week had gone by, we teachers went off in a little reconnaissance group. Suddenly, going through the gigantic savannah, we found ourselves face to face with a herd of elephants. We turned right back with big long strides, because until that day we had only ever been close to chickens and goats.

Shortly afterwards, we fortunately heard the news that here and there Batutsi herdsmen and Bahutu farmers got on well enough in the remote hills by the Burundi border. For a year, we bivouacked in a camp, sheltering from the elements in cabins fashioned out of cardboard with sheet metal roofs. To tell you the truth, we kept warm the frail hope that the situation would calm down, and that we would be able to return to our native lands. Alas, more and more Batutsi refugees, and bad news, kept coming in increasing quantities from different communes.

As we were surviving in spite of our poverty, the local

administration decided in the year 1961 to celebrate the first anniversary of the Republic's independence by authorising us to scatter out into the bush to claim plots. So we registered on a beneficiaries' list and when your number hit top of the list, you could go mark out two hectares of your choice, which was yours to clear for yourself.

Life was very difficult. We had to pull up shrubs in the dust, dig up a thick crust of earth with wooden tools, plant sorghum and banana trees, erect mud and palm huts. We had to defend ourselves against wild animals with the help of spears, bows and arrows, and sometimes sticks. Near my own plot, with my own eyes I saw lions, leopards, spotted hyenas and bison. There were no springs, and our stomachs were not accustomed to drinking the stagnant marsh water. So many of us died from typhus, dysentery, malaria. You had to harden your hands on the handle, working without letting up in the sun and the rain, bringing into the world ever more children in order to survive. Then we started to get results at the market. We sold a meagre crop destined for shops in Kigali; on our small savings, we were able to buy little herds of goats. Native Batutsis started offering us cows, out of good heartedness or in order to marry our prettiest girls.

All that time, we stayed in groups according to acquaintance. The hill of Ntarama was inhabited by newcomers from Ruhengeri, on the opposite slope were those from Byumba, lower down those from Gitarama. On the hill, we assembled as large families, or, to use your vocabulary, as tribes. And over the years, as later when the influx of Bahutu arrivals accelerated, they in turn did the same on other hills; and we did not really mix because of the distances. The Bahutus showed up above all because of directives issued by the Ministry of Agriculture, when high ranking civil servants had noticed that the Bugesera bush was being inhabited and farmed. It was in 1973 that the Bahutus became equal to the Batutsis in number. These Bahutus were strong, very hard-working, some came to settle

with savings; we were quickly on good terms with one another because we needed their money or their hands.

Between farmers, we hardly ever shared a beer together, but we talked politely and without reticence. We hailed from the same culture: beans, manioc, banana, yam, with the help of hoes and machetes. Bahutus were the better planters. As for the Batutsis, they reared cattle; contrary to Bahutus, who found such work irksome.

As there were not a great number of schools authorised to Batutsis, because of the admissions quota per commune, we teachers had our pupils sit down together in a circle in the shade of tall leafy trees and we improvised classes right there in the dust. In the Bugesera, the authorities and administration were Bahutu; the soldiers, the burgomaster, accountants and directors were also Bahutu. Therefore, the moment a Batutsi got hold of an education, he became a teacher and schooled Batutsi children.

This was how we teachers came to be very poorly seen by the authorities, who showed their jealousy. They did not dare silence us openly, but the moment killings began, teachers were placed top of the list, on the pretext that they were frequenting the *inkotanyi*. The *inkotanyi* were Batutsi rebels from the maquis of Burundi who launched attacks on Rwanda. Whenever there were *inkotanyi* attacks against Bahutus, the army went to kill Batutsis as punishment.

This is how it went. They killed in order, families of men who had gone to fight in Burundi; then teachers, for the motives I have already explained; then well-off farmers, to distribute their land and their grain to new Bahutu arrivals. One year it is burning hot, one year it was very calm. For example, 1963 was a year of a thousand murders, as a natural response to multiple rebel incursions. 1964 was a peaceful year, 1967 disastrous from the number of dead; in that year, the army flung hundreds of Tutsis alive into the Urwabaynanga, a mud swamp by the Burundi border, proof of which can still be fished out. In 1973, they even went as far as killing pupils in the classroom... The massacres were unpredictable. This is why, even when the situation seemed calm, the two eyes in your head never slept together.

Nevertheless, we Batutsis had chased the wild animals away, had conquered the tsetse, and had learned to obey the authorities. Despite our wrangles, villages multiplied, Batutsis continued as numerous as Bahutus and they owned more and more cows. Some Batutsis became a little rich, and Bahutus started working for them. Nyamata was quickly growing, shops were mixed, but the best stocked were Batutsi. *Cabarets* sprang up, and were immediately popular. Life was difficult but did not seem all that bad.

There were many excellent people amongst the Bahutus. I remember one day I was already tied to a tree facing a row of army rifles, because I bore the same tribal name as a maquis leader. There was nothing left to do but die, but I persisted in claiming my innocence. By chance, a captain, on a tour of inspection, saw me at death's door and to the soldiers cried out: "I know this man's voice. His name is Jean-Baptiste, from Cyugaro, he is a good teacher, and has nothing to do with the rebel commandos", and he had the ropes cut. This said, many Bahutus were more and more wary of Batutsis, because of the *inkotanyi*. And also because there were fewer and fewer plots to cultivate.

The discord grew venomous once the multiparty system was authorised in 1991. At meetings, discussions in public became all too dangerous. Debates got scalding hot, and you ran the risk of wounds each time. The *interahamwe* paraded along the roads and the paths and strutted about the cabarets. The radio called Batutsis cockroaches; at public meetings Bahutu politicians predicted the death of Batusis. They were terribly afraid of the *inkotanyi* or of foreign military invasion. I think that it was at this time that they started to contemplate genocide.

In 1992, they counted four hundred Batutsi corpses in the

forests, without a single reprimand from the chief of police. When the war started two years later, we were well accustomed to killings. I foresaw a routine tragedy, nothing more. I thought, "The situation is too explosive to go walking on the high road, but if we do not leave the hill, it will perhaps settle down." After the massacre in the church, I understood that things were deadly serious. That day, I joined a line of runaways for the marsh at Nyamwiza and I squatted down in the mud.

In the beginning, we hoped for help in the depth of the papyrus. But God himself showed that he had forgotten us, the Whites even more so. Later, all we could hope for was to reach the next day's dawn. Through the marsh, I saw women crawling through the mud without lamentations. I saw a sleeping infant lying forgotten on its mother who had been hacked. I heard people, with no more strength left in their muscles to walk, explaining that they wanted to eat corn one last time. Because they knew well they would be cut down the next day. I saw people's skin shrivelling up on the bone, week after week. I heard people humming tenderly to themselves to stave off the moans of their own death.

In the wood, I happened on news of the death of my brother's two children, who had passed the national entrance exam to university. In the marsh, I learned of the death of my wife, Domine Kabanyana, and my son, Jean-Sauveur. My second son died behind me as we ran through the marsh. Trapped in a surprise attack, we attempted to escape our pursuers. He tripped on a cluster of thorns, cried out, I heard the first blows, I was already far away. He was in the fourth year of primary school.

You must understand that if the rest of us, us runaways, lived at the bivouac in the evenings "all for one, one for all", during our flight through the marsh it was "everyone for himself". Except, of course, for mothers carrying their little children.

In the evening, we were four families to group together in

my house in Cyugaro. There were no more mats or mattresses to roll out on the floor because the *interahamwe* had stolen them. We would exchange a little conversation, above all about the details of that day, or some words of comfort. We did not argue. We teased no one; we did not mock the women who had been raped, because all the women expected to be raped. We were all fleeing from the same death, we suffered the same fate. Even yesterday's enemies could find no pretext for a quarrel, because in any case, it no longer served a purpose.

During that time, we talked a little as to the why of this accursed situation, and we kept coming up against the same replies. The Bugesera, formerly empty land, was now crammed with people. The authorities feared being chased out by the "Ugandan" RPF, the Bahutus gazed longingly on our land... But all this could not explain the extermination, no more than it can now.

I wish to point out an historical anomaly. History books of the Belgian colonisation taught us that Batwa pygmies were the first to inhabit Rwanda, with bows and arrows; then came the Bahutus, with hoes, then the Batutsis settled with cows, and grabbed hold of too much land because of their immense herds. But here, in our Bugesera region, the arrivals succeeded one another precisely in the opposite direction, because the Batutsi came first, as pioneering land clearers, with nothing in their hands. Nevertheless, the genocide in the Bugesera was as efficient as elsewhere. I therefore refute these historical explanations. I think that history as dictated by the colonists planned the Batutsis being shackled to the Bahutu yoke; a plan which, out of bad luck if I may say so, transformed itself into a genocide.

Today, I suffer from poverty in multiple ways. My wife is dead, I have lost my family, except for two children. I used to have six cows, ten goats, thirty hens, now my pen is empty. My immediate neighbour is dead, the man who offered me my first cow is dead. Of the nine teachers at the school, six were killed, two are in prison. After so many long years, it is difficult to become a true friend to new colleagues, when you have lost people who you were used to. I am remarried with one of my wife's little sisters; but I lead a life of no interest to me anymore. At night, I go through a life all too peopled with the many dead of my family, who as killed folk talk amongst themselves, and who ignore me and do not even look at me anymore. During the day, the pain of solitude is of another kind.

What happened in Nyamata, in the churches, in the marshes and the hills, are the supernatural doings of ordinary people. Let me tell you why I say this. The headmaster and the school inspector in my area took part in the killings, striking blows with spiked clubs. Two teacher colleagues with whom I used to exchange beers and pupil assessments got stuck in too, if I may put it like this. A priest, the magistrate, the assistant chief of police, a doctor, killed with their own hands.

These intellectuals had never lived in the time of the Batutsi kings. They had never been robbed of anything nor bullied, they were under obligation to no one. They wore pleated cotton pants, they had proper time to rest, drove around in vehicles or on mopeds. Their wives wore jewels and knew city ways, their children frequented white schools.

These learned people were calm, and they rolled up their sleeves to get a firm grip on a machete. So for people like me who have taught the Humanities their life long, criminals such as these are a terrible mystery.

6

At the widows' corner

The primary school at Cyugaro, rebuilt in brick, today has some twenty-five classes in which Hutu and Tutsi pupils sit together on the same benches. In the village, most earth houses have fissures or are collapsing, the waste land is invading gardens. Five kilometres separate the school from the marsh. The only trail crosses manioc fields, passes the walls of two burned out villas. *Iwuwa*, trees with yellow flowers, and *umuko*, trees with red flowers, adorn the savannah through which gangs of children roam looking for wild cabbage. Then the track plunges into a forest of eucalyptus, luminous because of the height of the trees.

On the other side of the wood reappears the green immensity. You tear down a steep slope and, behind a fringe of wild banana trees, you come to the swamps. Your first impression is one of an inextricable tangle of papyrus and reeds gone rotten in the water. It's possible nevertheless to enter it by pushing the tangled stems out of the way. The ground, spongy during the dry season, muddy in the wet, smells of putrid mud. With each step, you are up to your shins in mud. A droning of flies, mosquitoes and dragonflies serves as background noise to the melodious laughter of the ibis and the piercing screams of macaques and black talapoins, whose aerobatics you can just make out. If you're patient, you can also stop and listen to the grunts of invisible wild hogs, or to the swishing of slender sitatungas, marsh antelope, in the tall grass.

Coming out of the marsh, we come across a fifteen year old boy, a load of turf on his back. Every afternoon, he goes deep into the swamp hunting waterfowl or gathering turf. He invites us into his adobe house, surrounded by a palm enclosure, which, set on a hillock, dominates this papyrus expanse. His name is Jean-Claude Khadafi. He offers us some *urwagwa* in wooden bowls, goes to have a look at his ditch filled with ripening bananas, sits at the edge of it and recounts the genocide. At the time, his house sheltered fugitives too old and without the energy to go up the hill to the school in Cyugaro, who sometimes had given up hiding in the mud and wanted to spend one last day under a roof, waiting for the killers who, without fail, would come and finish them off. Many such people inhabit Jean-Claude's memories.

Today, he lives with his father, the only other family survivor, gone wandering off since dawn into the forest, from which he will return in the evening without saying a word, as he does every day. Jean-Claude prefers the remoteness of his house here, amidst eucalyptus and papyrus, to making a home in a new house on the Nelson Mandela estate at the edge of the track, near school and friends. He explains that not a day goes by that he doesn't go into the marshes, that neither heat waves nor bouts of malaria can stop him from going. In fact, his gaze is never long away from the flat green plain that rustles unexpectedly.

From his home, a brush path joins the junction at Kanzenze. The village used to bustle with its lively market. Today it's just a minibus stop. A little off the track is Marie Mukarulinda's *cabaret*, a time honoured meeting point for business deals. The room is painted an African green, peeling and faded like all public rooms. The seats have seen better days, crates of Primus and Fanta are stacked against the wall.

You notice Marie for her beanpole figure. In the mornings, she works in the field. In the evenings, she tries to save her late husband's *cabaret*, with a management policy of utter simplicity, since money, which only comes in every now and then from clients paying for beer, is immediately used to buy a drink for a regular fallen on hard times. The backyard outside is Pétronille's smoky domain, a large lady who herself is a widow and Marie's inseparable accomplice, who on a brazier lovingly cooks the most delicious goat brochettes in the Bugesera.

Marie's *cabaret* is called the Widows' Corner because many women from the environs, almost all of them widows since the genocide, like to meet here to share one or several bottles of Primus, a good excuse to go on chatting for ever, and to laugh at everything and anything, and at themselves above all. Today, for example, a vet has come from Kigali to supervise the artificial insemination of a herd of goats. Invited to the *cabaret* after his visit, he is hauled over by Marie's girlfriends who demand he comes back again to look after them too. He freezes, dumbfounded, until a collective explosion of laughter puts him at his ease and he feels compelled, for his pains, to buy everyone a round.

In one corner of the veranda, seated on a stool on his own, you notice the stiff and thin figure of a man with an impeccably clean shaven face, a combed grey moustache, dressed up in a threadbare double-breasted black suit several times patched up. This is Monsieur Gaspard. He is the neighbourhood patriarch, whose distinction is rivalled only by the accuracy of his eighty-year-old memory. The sole survivor from a family of twelve, Gaspard bears his solitude with dignity. Without the slightest hint of complaint, he admits that he is now only waiting for the end of his life in the company of misery and melancholy, between a chair in his hovel nearby, and a stool at Marie's cabaret, looking at a bottle of beer which neighbours surreptitiously put before him, and which he savours very slowly. By way of saying goodbye, he quotes a Rwandan proverb in Kinyarwandan: *Amarina y'umugabo atemba ajya mu unda* which means: A man's tears flow in his belly.

A few kilometres further on, towards Nyamata, in a clearing, three houses stand at the edge of the track. Angélique

Mukamanzi has been settled in one of them, the property of an exiled Hutu peasant, waiting for the repairs to the house on her family plot to be finished. Angélique is a girl who makes it a point of honour never to wear cloths or dresses but only black pants, "country-style" denim jackets and "European-look" shirts. Returning from the fields or the market, she hurriedly varnishes her nails, slips into sandals or pumps, in time to spend the end of the afternoon leaning against the wall of neighbouring houses as if she were expecting a date to show up. Recently, she met a sweetheart who was good-looking, attentive and funny, an agronomist by trade. Only, she says, not without an ironic smile, she felt she had to break it off when she realised he was Hutu.

During the genocide, as the days went by in the marshes, she inherited a small group of orphans, becoming, whether she liked it or not, big sister, adoptive mother, the family head.

Angélique Mukamanzi

25 years old, farmer
Hill of Rwankeli (Musenyi)

With my sister Laetitia, I today look after eight little non-accompanied children. It came about naturally. In the marshes, when the parents went away to their deaths without taking their children along with them, those like us who did not have any offered to replace them on the spot. Later, time entrusted them to us forever.

Before the war, I studied diligently because I wanted to take the national exam in Kigali and land a beautiful career for myself. I was very well regarded by the boys, life seemed good. At school I had a mix of friends, Tutsi and Hutu. The latter never had a bad word to say. I felt my first pangs of fear when people started leaving the Bugesera after the skirmishes of 1992. On the road then more and more dark words began to be heard. This is also why I wished to turn myself towards the capital.

Three days after the plane crash, a small company of us moved into the church at Ntarama: my family and neighbouring folk, with bundles of what we needed to survive. During the day, the courageous ventured out into the surrounding fields to bring back some food. At night, we slept inside or outside, according to who was weak or fit. When the *interahamwe* encircled the fencing, men began letting stones fly so as to slow down their advance. The women gathered the stones, because they did not want to die any old way. But our resistance did not have much vigour behind it. Grenades exploded at the front door. I was positioned at the back, I raced down the slope, I ran so fast I forgot about breathing for an hour, then dived into the marsh *urunfunzo*, which I knew by reputation. *Urunfunzo* are papyrus trees. At this moment, I did not of course have any idea that for the next month I was going to spend my days in the mud, covered from head to toe, under the tyranny of the mosquitoes.

The killers worked in the swamps from nine to four, half past four, as the sun would have it. Sometimes, if it rained too much, they came later in the morning. They came in columns, announcing their arrival with songs and whistles. They beat drums, they sounded very cheerful to be going killing for an entire day. One morning, they would take one path, the next day another path. When we heard the first whistles, we disappeared in the opposite direction. One morning, they cheated, they came from all sides springing traps and ambushes; and that day was a very dispiriting one because we knew that that evening there would be more than the usual number of dead.

In the afternoon they would not sing anymore because they were tired, but chatting away, they returned to their homes. They fortified themselves with drink and by eating the cows that they slaughtered at the same time as the Tutsis. These were truly very calm and accomplished killings. If the RPF liberators had delayed one week more on the road, there would not be a single Bugesera Tutsi left living to deny the lies, such as the criminals' so-called drunkenness.

In the evening, after the killings, we scattered out into the night to dig in fields, collecting manioc and beans. It was also the banana season. We ate raw for a month, hands filthy with mud, like louts. It was the same fate for adults as for little children, who no longer had the opportunity to drink maternal milk or other nutritious substances. So, many people, even though not struck by machetes, were sprung by a deadly weakness. In the morning, we woke and we found them, lying beside us, stiffened in their sleep. And we, without a word of farewell for them, without a last gift from time, were unable to cover them decently.

We made the most of rainy nights by rubbing ourselves down with palm leaves, cleaning away the thickest coatings of refuse and the mud filth. Then we lay down on the ground. We talked of the day, wondered who had died that day, asked ourselves who was to die the next. We discussed the evil fate that had fallen on our heads. We did not exchange many words of joy, but many despondent ones.

In the morning, we could not even give ourselves a little moment to dry out in the rising sun. We went off again, soaked through, to deposit the children in little groups under the cover of the papyrus. We told them to stay as nice as fish in ponds – meaning not to put more than a head out of the water and not to cry. We gave them muddy water to drink, even if it were sometimes tinged with blood. Then, in our turn, we covered ourselves in mud. Sometimes, we could glimpse one another through the surrounding foliage. We asked ourselves why God had forsaken us here, in the midst of snakes, which fortunately did not bite anyone.

One night, my heart bled from a wound that will never ever scar over. Coming out of my hiding place in the evening, I saw that they had caught Maman. She lay floating in the mud. Her name was Marthe Nyirababji. Papa and Godmother and the rest

of the family were killed shortly afterwards, on the terrible 30th of April. Papa was called Ferdinand Muduevu. He was run through by a Hutu neighbour who danced and sang over him. After this, I had to join another team of survivors from the hill. Through the papyrus branches, my eyes met those of an *interahamwe* who was killing nearby. I saw many people cut beside me, all the time I fought down a tenacious fear, truly an all too great terror. I overcame it, but I am not saying it has left me forever.

At the end of the genocide, I was settled for three months in Nyamata, lower down in the commune, in an abandoned hut. I should have been contented, but I was still too alarmed and too tired. We felt out of sorts; we were demoralised, we were embarrassed by what we had become. I think that we did not truly believe in deliverance.

Deep down, we thought that we would never be saved from those who had threatened us and weeks went by before we gave ourselves up to cheerfulness. Every day I walked an hour to get to the family farm. I took up the hoe to give the children food to eat. I moulded bricks out of clay to build a new temporary house with the help of a mason sent by the commune.

At present, waiting for our roof to go up, I live in the house of a Hutu who has not returned from the Congo. I place all my hopes in a programme to set up a small business selling rice, sugar and salt in the main street near the chemist. You get used to work, but not to regrets.

Before the war, I had decided to turn away from village life, as I cherished studying so much. If the genocide had not overwhelmed us, perhaps I would have passed the national exam, I would have clinched my diploma in law, and I would be dressed in lawyer's robes in a private practice in Kigali. But today I am twenty-five years old. All I can see are obstacles to my life, marshes around my memories, and a hoe holding its handle out to me. I do not know which way my head should turn to find a husband anymore. I could not confide in a Hutu man anymore, I am not necessarily hoping for a survivor. I have forgotten the fantasy of love. I am simply waiting for an everyday man with gentle eyes that alight upon me for what I am. I hear candidates knocking on the door and introducing themselves wearing brushed shoes, but I see no one anymore, neither to the left nor right, who could provide me with tenderness.

Many Hutu families have returned to the hills, even though their men are in prison. For them, the commune opens wide the doors to their homes. Some completely disagreed with what happened, others fully supported it. These families work their plots amongst themselves; they hardly speak to us, they do not return anything that they looted, they do not ask for pardon. Their silence makes me feel very uncomfortable. I am sure I have recognised some criminals' faces amongst these families working in the fields. They have kept muscular arms fit for cultivating. My sister and I have only slender arms to feed the orphans. I do not think it's realistic to only entrust time and silence with the difficult mission of reconciliation.

In Ntarama, survivors are becoming bad or desperate. They say, "I had a strong husband, I had a house with durable walls, I had beautiful children, I had big cows, I worked every day and the day after that, all for nothing." Many are the men and women who no longer bother. They drink Primus the minute they have a few pennies and they don't give a damn about anything; they get drunk on alcohol and bad memories. There are those who draw pleasure in always talking of the same fatal moments they lived through. As if that is what they need now.

To listen to them, I deduce that in time people will not remember the genocide in the same way. For example, a neighbouring woman talks of how her maman died in the church; then, two years later, she explains that her maman died in the marsh. For me, there is no lie. The girl had an acceptable reason to wish for her mother's death to have taken place in the church. Perhaps because she abandoned her running full stretch through the marsh and was ashamed. Perhaps because it relieved her of an all too painful sorrow; to persuade herself that her maman in this way suffered less, one fatal blow on the first day. Then time offered the girl a little peace, so she could remember the truth, and she accepted it.

Another girl denies that she was wounded, even though her arms show eye-catching scars. But one day she hears someone talk of a sexual attack; then in her turn she dares to tell of her own sexual attack, and to what she owes the miracle of her life. She has not lied either, she was only waiting for the company of adversity so as to reveal a painful truth.

There are also people who never stop altering the details of a fateful day because they think that on that day their lives garnered the luck of another equally deserving life. Despite these zig zags though, personal recollections are not forgotten, thanks to conversations in small assemblies. People choose certain memories, according to their character, and they relive them as if they happened last year, and will happen for the next hundred years.

People claim that the differences between Hutus and Tutsis are an invention. I cannot understand such nonsense because once the massacres began in the Bugesera there was not a single Tutsi who could have stayed alive one little hour out in the wide open amongst the Hutus. But I do not want to explain anything as to this difference or the so-called misunderstanding between the two ethnic groups. I believe we should be granted an appropriate justice, and by that I do not want to say that the prisoners should be shot. Nor do I wish to express my thoughts as to why the Whites watched the massacres with their arms folded. I believe that Whites make the most of it when Blacks get at each other so they can then sow the seeds of their own ideas, and that is all. I do not want to say anything about what I can glimpse in the hearts of the Hutus.

I simply say that Hutu neighbours agreed to exterminate their Tutsi neighbours in the swampland, to loot their houses, to ride their bicycles, to eat their cows.

I now see this desolate time which passes before me as an enemy. I suffer from being tied down to this life here, which is not the one that was destined for me. Amongst neighbours, when we ask ourselves why the genocide chose this little blot of Rwanda on the map of Africa, we go far off into discussions which get all tied up in knots and which never conclude in an answer all can agree upon.

7

Bicycle-taxis under an
acacia tree

A petrol station, meeting place for tyre repair men,
marks the beginning of Nyamata's main street. It's
redder and much wider than the track it prolongs. It's rocky and
potholed on one side, where vehicles pass, sandy on the other,
which is reserved for pedestrians. Opposite the petrol pumps,
waste ground serves as a bus station for "Dubai" minibuses and
trucks to pick up passengers, goats and bundles.

At the beginning of Main Street you pass a religious
bookshop, the ruins of Bugesera Club and the old football team's
HQ, Chez Clémentine's – the first joint where you can drink
banana wine. Take any alleyway to the right, you go past small
courtyards and little houses thronged with kids and then
immediately come out into the fields. If you take a street to the
left, you come to the Pentecostal church whose open-air choral
recitals – refined, exuberant, sometimes hysterical – provide
incredible musical moments. If you go straight you're in the
town centre, at the market square.

In Nyamata the first two-storey villa, a Burundian merchant's
project, has not yet got past the foundations. In the streets
there's only one private car left, a white Suzuki belonging to
another tradesman. The cars the town used to be jammed with,
all destroyed or taken away during the exodus, have in fact yet to
be replaced. The few vehicles kicking up dust in the main street
are shopkeepers' vans – also requisitioned for funeral processions, marriages, sporting events – and 4X4 vehicles which are

either the commune's or belong to humanitarian organisations. So people go around in carts drawn by bulls harnessed to unusual aluminium yokes, or on Japanese monocylinder motorbikes, and most often of course on foot or bike.

The main bicycle-taxi rank can be found at a corner of the market square where, in the shade of a mimosa in full bloom, around thirty cyclists wait for clients while listening to the radio. A nearby hut serves as a workshop for bike mechanics, often knee high to a grasshopper, who repair wheels and pedals with the dexterity of magicians.

These black bikes are mostly Boda Bodas with large wheels, and sausage tyres more or less grooved depending on usage. They are sometimes fitted with front shock absorbers, and always with brake blocks operated by levers fixed to the bottom of the frame. Comfortable leather saddles mounted on three enormous springs provide gyroscopic suspension ideal for cushioning rides over potholes. The handlebars are fitted with melodious bells, luminous reflector stripes. Chrome and accessories depend on the model. Some are decorated with golden friezes, others protected by a sunshade or fitted with a front seat. Some enjoy an anti-theft lock, a looking glass or a framed holy image. Bicycle taxis carriers are padded out with a detachable leather cushion to alternatively allow for the transport of clients or goods.

The other taxi ranks are located near the hospital, at the cattle fair on Tuesdays and, at the end of the school day, beside the English-speaking lycee. The fare for a trip in town varies from three to five francs. Fares for longer trips through the woods require some friendly haggling.

Messenger and delivery boys also work with bicycles. Everything – messages or sacks of flour, trunks, furniture, goats, petrol jerry cans – can be transported by bike. At nightfall, when it's time for a Primus in the fading light, delivery boys criss-cross streets, going from warehouse to *cabaret*, bearing stacks of beer crates on their carriers, held there by an infallible combination of elastic straps.

Near the main street, in yards where pots of *foufou* are steaming, two small screening rooms advertised by posters show videos on a crackling screen at even-numbered hours. Jean-Claude Van Damme films compete with Sylvester Stallone's Rambos. Since the dancehalls were destroyed, young people now listen to music around hairdressing salons called One Love, Chez les Sportifs, and Texas. On the main street, you can still find a dozen chemists, three out of four photo salons, a health centre, a baker called Au Bon Pain Quotidien, a butcher's called Butcher but no hi-fi shop, no fashion boutique and, most surprisingly for an African town, no jeweller.

The main street is never empty. It plays host to civil servants on their midday break. After classes, schoolgirls in navy blue dresses, schoolboys in khaki uniform, high school boys in white shirts, give it colour, as does a vast array of red, yellow, green, and blue diamond-shaped parasols, on market days. It suddenly empties at kick-off during football matches in the stadium at the end of the street and is crowded again at half-time. To compensate for the lack of telephones, you go to the main street and pick up and give the latest news.

Innocent Rwiliza, who dreads having to confront so many shades back at home, is one of the main street's most popular mainstays. Ten years studying in the hills and fifteen years teaching in town means he knows everyone. He is secretary to the school inspection board and the founder of several mutual aid associations. He's one of the twenty heroic survivors from the forest of Kayumba. He belongs to no clan but is behind every helping hand; he mocks with tenderness, expresses ideas with gentleness, becomes nervous only when you talk about the church, where his first wife perished. Epiphanie, his second, has already given him four children.

He drinks Primus only – one, two, five bottles as our meetings dictate – which he asks for lukewarm. Any other beer, or any variation in temperature, which he immediately detects on touching the bottle, or any other drink for that matter, would make him instantly sick. He's curious about everything, about people and foreign countries, but focuses his intelligence – desperately, he knows – on trying to understand what he's been through. One of his dreams is to write a book about the genocide, but he claims he has neither the time nor the energy yet. In the meantime he chats about it, debates it, jokes about it, a lot, with everyone; not just because he doesn't want to forget anything, not just because he wants to understand, but because talking also does him good.

Innocent Rwililiza

38 years old, teacher
Nyamata town centre

My father was a veterinarian's assistant in Ruhengeri. He was sent with many others to fertilise a plot on the hill of Kanombe. Which is what he did with his own two hands. In Rwanda, farming is not something that can be taught; it comes to you. If no better business awaits you for the while, then you pick up the hoe and you go dig in the fields.

At the time when my parents crossed the Nyabarongo river, a few Hutu natives were already scattered here and there in the bush, and were not at all wicked. They knew nothing of the chaos fermenting throughout the rest of the country and they looked on the refugees with very peaceable eyes.

In Kanombe, there were only us two brothers and two sisters. We lived in a straw hut. We had to walk twenty kilometres through the bush every day to get to school. On Sundays we had to clear the land. I went from primary through to secondary school and I became a teacher. I married, and settled with my wife in Nyamata's town centre because in the hills the plots were full to the brim.

At the time, Nyamata already deserved to be called more

than a village, with a respectable market and a solid brick church. The streets were in constant flux, houses had sprung up very quickly. You came across shops of all sorts, a minibus terminal to Kigali, *cabarets* selling local drinks and export beers, a secondary school, a very moderately-priced hotel, a cultural centre nicely set off with a lawn. Nyamata bore all the promise of becoming a town, there was even talk of a commune, in spite of the threat of droughts. There were barely more Tutsis than Hutus, we felt at ease.

It was afterwards, around 1992, that politics came and spoiled everything. Militia and politicians came from Kigali sending out signals of dark portent. A Hutu burgomaster was even killed because he refused to give chase to Tutsis. Amongst ourselves, we no longer mixed with Hutus at the same *cabarets* for fear of coming back wounded, but we still spoke with civility to one another at work and on the road. In 1994 I could smell, like everyone else, a catastrophe cooking. You no longer dared enter such and such a *cabaret* if you were not a member of such and such a party. We Tutsis limited ourselves to going to Tutsi shops to drink our Primus without any problems.

I remember one evening, a few weeks before the attacks, I was returning home from work in the company of a Hutu neighbour and colleague. We were talking of what was being negotiated at the Arusha summit between the government and the rebels, and of our political worries. Half-way home, he stopped, looked at me and said: "Innocent, you are going to be exterminated." I retorted: "No, I do not think so. We are going to suffer once again, but doubtless we shall survive." He repeated to me: "Innocent, listen to me, I must tell you that you are all going to die." I later happened upon this colleague in the neighbourhood, riding along in an army van from the camp at Gako, pointing out the houses of people who had to be killed. He spotted me and then got on with his job.

The day after Habyarimana's plane crashed, we continued teaching in the daytime but for fear of underhand tricks, slept

far from our homes in the bush at night. On the morning of the
11th of April, there was a great commotion in town. Soldiers
had started doing some very serious shooting in the streets. But
quickly these soldiers noticed that there was no threat coming
from the people, and they no longer used up their cartridges,
they then only gave a helping hand to the *interahamwe* – who
had already rushed in to start thumping. They started with
prosperous shopkeepers first, because even then they were
above all preoccupied with getting rich.

In the panic, a crowd rushed to the town hall. We stayed two
hours or so in the courtyard, waiting for words of reassurance.
Then the burgomaster came out, dressed in his blue ceremonial
costume. He declared: "If you go back home, you shall be killed.
If you escape into the bush, you shall be killed. If you stay here,
you shall be killed. Nevertheless, you must leave here, because I
do not want any blood in front of my town hall."

Women, children, and the weakest began walking to the
church. As for me, I said to myself: "Things are completely out
of hand. They are going to kill there too for sure, and in any
case I do not want to die in a church." Which is the reason why
I ran all day without destination. I spent the night in the
undergrowth and the next day reached Kayumba. Up there, two
or three kilometres from the town, there were about six
thousand of us in good health, waiting in the eucalyptus forest
to see how events would unfold.

On the day of the massacre in the church, from up in
Kayumba you could hear the grenades and see the smoke. My
wife and child had taken refuge inside. In the wood four days
later, I crossed paths with a maman who had escaped the
massacre. She said to me: "Innocent, I come bringing bad news
– I happened upon your wife in the affray in the church. In the
state I left her, I must tell you is that she is no longer of this
world." I was stunned, but I still hoped. I said to myself: "If
no one has seen her remains, then she may have escaped too."

Even today, years later, when I spy a figure in the distance that looks like her, I jump out of my skin in the middle of the street. It is very harrowing to live in false hope. I can tell you today that to survive with the memory of a wife and a child, when you do not know how they were killed, when you have not seen them dead, and when you have not buried them, is the most dispiriting thing of all.

I could not have brought my wife and my son up to the hill of Kayumba, because they could not run fast enough. I did not follow them to the church which by custom was reserved for the weakest persons. I said to myself: "Since you are going to die, you must nevertheless try and last two or three days longer." This is why we parted ways.

But there is another reason, a little delicate to explain, as to why we separated; and which I owe to myself to add. Here goes. When everyone in a family must die, and when there is nothing you can do to save your wife or alleviate her sufferings, and the same for her too, it is better to go get killed elsewhere. I explain myself more clearly. If you are not going to die first, if you are going to hear your papa, your maman, your wife and your children scream, and you are unable to lift a hand to save them, even to help them die a better death, then you shall die in your own turn amidst the destruction of feelings you had for one another when times were good, because you will feel too guilty about a situation which was completely out of your control. A terrible feeling of shame will engulf you at that last moment and have the better of love, fidelity, and all such sentiments as these. At the edge of life, memories of even the best moments with her will be confiscated. This is why I thought that it might be better to be cut down each to his own, out of sight of the other.

On the hill of Kayumba, the situation immediately became sombre. It is a eucalyptus forest as I have already pointed out. Eucalyptus are tall trees which grow too widely apart for there to be any hope of hiding amongst them, unlike the dense papyrus in the marshes. So the bottom of the hill was encircled by *interahamwe*. In the morning they came up in rows, singing, and then, shouting, they began their pursuit. To have any hope of escaping them, you needed to be able to do a hundred metre dash in nine seconds. You had to slip through the trees, you had to duck and dive all day without ever slowing down.

They often organised ambushes. They would conceal themselves somewhere, in silence, then their colleagues would turn up behind like beaters driving antelope to the places where they – the cheats – were hiding. And so they killed even more of us. Like safaris in Kilimanjaro, without the cameras. So you had to run without ever letting alertness dwindle, and you had to acquire a certain technique as follows.

As I have told you, the *interahamwe* were cunning. So you needed even more cunning counter-tactics. When we heard them coming up the hill, since they were shouting and singing as they went, we let them approach as close as two hundred metres. At that distance, there is no danger from an arrow. So you pretended to run away, all the time circling them at very high speed. They kept pursuing those who did not have enough speed, and who were fleeing straight ahead; and so you, now at their backs, had earned a very beneficial rest. After two or three hours, a new line of attack came up to finish off the wounded; and you circled round them again. This was how young people with nimble legs that sliced through the air tried to save themselves. As for the others, they had no chance but to run straight ahead, breathless, trying not to get massacred before the day was done.

At around four o'clock, the evil-doers went back to town, because they feared the dark. In the evening, from up on the hill, we could hear them rejoicing with songs and drinking. We could see that they were now living in the most comfortable houses. With the breeze, we could sometimes even smell grilling meat. While we went to scour the fields and sleep in the rain, sheltering beneath branches.

The next morning, they would come back up the hill

singing, and the hunt resumed for the rest of the day. We tried to run together in small teams, to inspire courage in one another. He who was surprised in an ambush, was killed; he who twisted his ankle, was killed; he who was caught by fever or diarrhoea, was killed. Every evening, the forest was strewn with dozens of the dead and dying.

But we were doubly unfortunate on the hill because, even though it was the great rain season, we could find nothing to drink for the lack of containers. In the beginning, we were able to slake our thirst off corrugated metal roofs. After this, though, they made off with the roofs to fortify their own houses in town, so we no longer knew how to collect water. Except by licking wet leaves. Unlike our compatriots in the marshes, we did not have access to water. So by the end of a day's racing, he who had saved himself, the minute he thought to make the most of his freedom break, immediately felt dehydrated. In fact, in the middle of the rainy season, more and more people were just dying of thirst.

In the forest, we stuck together by acquaintance or fate. We were covered in mud because we could no longer clean ourselves. There were mamans who had lost their cloths, girls who wrapped underwear around their heads to protect themselves from the sun. There were some suffering from festering wounds. When we regained peace and quiet again in the evenings, we sat down beside each other, picking the lice off and scrubbing each other's skin. But we never felt humiliated about this. We all had the same burden to bear and we never crossed paths with anyone else with whom we could compare our filthiness. Sometimes, we even found ways to tease one another. A maman would be seated beside you, delousing you, and would say: "Oh, you are so dirty we cannot even be sure you are black anymore," or some such joke. The only thing that mattered was to save yourself a little longer.

Sometimes, on the hill, we watched the Hutus partying in Nyamata, as they would have at a wedding. And we ended up saying aloud: "If only they would let us live up here, like animals, for the rest of our lives, without killing us though, it would be very acceptable. Let them take our houses, let them kill our cows, it is nothing. If they were to stop killing us, this would be fine."

Man conceals mysterious reasons for wishing to go on surviving. The more we died, the more ready we were to die, and yet the faster we ran to gain an extra moment of life. Even people who had their arms or legs cut would ask for water so as to last one hour more. I cannot explain this phenomenon. It is not an animal reflex; because an animal wants to go on living because it is not sure it is going to die, because it does not know what death means. For us, it was our one burning, singular, desire, if I may put it so clumsily.

But I think that for the Hutus, to see us so, living like the lowest of the lowest wildlife, it made the work easier. Especially for those who were not spurred to massacre out of hatred.

One day, we were in a group, and we surprised three Hutus. They had been distracted, and they had left themselves isolated. We encircled them, and they sat in the middle, upon leaves. Amongst us, there was one fellow who ran up to them with a handful of arrows picked up from the ground. We explained, "Alright, the tables have turned; this time it is for us to kill you with arrows." An old man begged us: "No, no, sorry, do not kill us." I said to him, "Oh really, and why so? You spend your days cutting us and now you cry so that no one shall run you through?" He said to me: "It is not my fault. It is the commune that desires it. Down there, they have been forcing us to do all this." I asked him: "If this is true, why do you never think only of coming up and spending the day in the shade, not killing anyone until evening comes, then returning well-rested to Nyamata and still well regarded by the powers that be?" He answered: "This is a good idea, I did not think of it." Very angry, I began shouting: "You did not think that you did not have to kill us?" He answered: "No, the more we kill, the more we forget to have any respect for you."

I believe now that this Hutu nurtured no ferocity in his heart. While we, on the other hand, bolted at the slightest noise, we scrabbled through the earth on our bellies in search of manioc, the lice guzzled us, we died cut by machetes like goats in the market. We looked like animals, since we no longer resembled the humans we used to be, and they had grown accustomed to see us as animals. They tracked us down as such. In truth, it was they who had become animals. They removed all humanity from the Tutsis so as to kill them at their ease, but in doing so they became worse than animals of the bush, because they no longer knew why they killed, and they did so with quirks. When an *interahamwe* caught a pregnant woman, he would start by piercing her belly with the help of a blade. Not even the spotted hyena could dream up such cruelty with his fangs.

In the forest of Kayumba, we lived united. We had nothing to steal from each other, nothing to squabble over. People who had never previously got on forget any problems that existed between them. I remember two loud flare-ups. One because of a huge man who growled wickedly the moment you came near his pot of food. Another was the fault of a young man, who insulted his sister and refused to feed her because she was clumsy at foraging in the fields. Two nasty pieces of work out of thousands of people, not enough to get worked up over.

When we slept one next to the other, even when we lay naked to wash our shorts, we had no urges to start groping at one another; we did not think about sex and its fantasies, because we had seen too much blood during the day. Together we were suffering the same fate, we faced the same danger and, since we had to die, we tried to remain good friends for as long as possible. There are days when I say to myself that if men and women could live on earth, as kind to one another as we had been in Kayumba, then the world would be such a more clement place than it is. But all these people who showed solidarity are dead, and they have not even been buried.

In the commune today, we know of Hutus who were forced to kill their Tutsi family so as to escape death themselves. But only one case of a Tutsi who killed Tutsis to try and save himself, one person out of several tens of thousands of people. This fellow was a much hailed player for Bugesera Sport, the local football team; he wanted to convert himself into an *interahamwe*; he denounced his neighbours, he helped to kill, to try and save himself by the grace of his footballing colleagues. The *interahamwe* used him for their ends and then, at the end of all ends, slew him in the middle of a road.

We knew that there was no point in offering the *interahamwe* our services as accomplices because they did not need them – they foresaw no exceptions. Even the girls preserved so as to be raped or used for as servants for domestic chores were captured by ordinary Hutus, because when the *interahamwe* noticed them, they were in a hurry to cut them without asking the owners. I know only of two girls in Nyamata who survived a stay in a killer's family. I cannot speak for those who may have been well hidden.

The Hutus were very determined to see our extermination through to the end. When one of us was caught, we never betrayed one other, because we knew it could not save us. He who offered to betray an acquaintance's hiding place could well be cut most cruelly, by way of thanks, to make them laugh. So we often died without even speaking, without protesting, except for the inevitable screams through the pain. As if we had become accustomed to death before being slaughtered.

One day, I remember I was hiding behind a ruin. Some *interahamwe* walked inside and found a family. I heard the blows striking bones, but I could barely hear any lamentations. Next, they discovered a child behind a well. It was a little girl. They set to cut her. From my hiding place I could listen to everything. She did not ask for pity to try and save herself; she only murmured before dying: "Jesus" I believe, or something like that, then little cries.

So why did they chop people up instead of killing them straightaway? I do not think it was to punish them for having tried to escape. Nor to discourage the living from running, from fleeing from the assassins all day long, saving themselves any way they could. Or perhaps they did so for a tiny percentage only. Whatever the case, these villains thought they would end it for us.

They chopped us out of a taste for barbarity, nothing more. Amongst them there were normal Hutus who killed normally, wicked Hutus who killed wickedly – most often *interahamwe*; and finally there were extremists in wickedness who killed with extreme wickedness.

Every morning, even on Sundays, the hunters came up various paths, they wore hats on their heads, carried machetes on their shoulders; they sang. In the evening, around four o'clock, they left, chatting as they went, leaving behind them one hundred, two hundred corpses beneath the eucalyptus. First the old and children, then the sick and the ailing, then women and the unlucky. Several teams tried to escape at night to Burundi. There are only two survivors left. One a burly herdsman who killed the man who was killing him, and who the next minute, without having noticed, found himself in Burundi. And Théoneste, who slipped through the bush thanks to a thousand herdsmen's tricks.

In Kayumba, there is talk of suicide some evenings. Ancients who had lived through too many threats since 1959, and who found that this was enough. Young people who wanted to avoid the machete, who preferred to die at the bottom of the waters and in their pain not beg the killers for mercy. But cases such as these were much rarer than in the marshes. On one hand, because we saw enough dead during the day, so as not to add to them. On the other hand, because there was nothing handy to kill yourself with. One single time though, a day of sorrow, I decided to put an end to it all and fling myself into the Nyabarongo River. On the way there, a group of *interahamwe* surged forward and altered my itinerary; in some ways I owe them my life.

In Kayumba, suicide demanded great bravery, energy and luck. But there were mamans and papas who, one day, refused to run. One morning, I was behind a rock in the company of a maman who was still young and vigorous. We heard the ruckus of the approaching murderers, I got up, she remained seated. I said to her, "Hurry up, or they will come upon." She quietly answered: "Go, Innocent. This time I shan't move." I ran; when I returned to the rock that evening, her head was sliced off.

In the end, there were only us sprinters left. We had begun as five or six thousand; one month later, when the *inkotanyi* arrived, there were twenty of us alive. That's the arithmetic. If the *inkotanyi* had lingered on the road one week more, our exact number would be zero. And all the Bugesera would be a desert, because the Hutus had grown so accustomed to killing they would have gone on and started killing each other too.

To those who equivocate on the Rwandan genocide I would simply like to draw their attention to the fact that if the Hutus had not been so worried about getting rich, they would have succeeded in exterminating every Tutsi in the country. It was our good luck that they wasted much time pulling down sheet metal roofs, searching houses and squabbling over the spoils. Also, when *interahamwe* landed a good haul, they threw a party; they ate to buck themselves up, they drank, they smoked to ease digestion, and they took the next day off.

Many foreign journalists say that beer and such things played a decisive role in the killings. This is correct, but in a way completely different to how they imagined it. In a certain way, many amongst us owe our survival to Primus and we should thank it. I will explain myself. The killers would turn up sober in the morning to start killing. But in the evening they would empty more Primuses than usual, to reward themselves, and that would soften them up for the next day. The more they killed, the more they stole, the more they drank. Perhaps to relax, to forget, or to congratulate themselves. In any case, the more they chopped, the more they drank in the evening, the more their schedule was delayed. Without a doubt, it is trifles such as looting and drunkenness that saved us.

As for us, the survivors of Kayumba, we engage in diverse occupations. Time moves us apart, but we continue to visit one another, we force ourselves to encourage one another, we evoke the bravery we showed up there. Those who frequent the *cabarets* share a Primus and chat about it. We still cannot explain what happened to us.

In Africa, I see that the more ethnic groups there are, the more people talk about them, the less of a problem they present. Wherever in the world one may be, whether you are white, or black, from the North Pole or the jungle, you do not inspire a contagious embarrassment. Here, in Rwanda, to be Hutu or Tutsi is quite a business. At the market, a Hutu can spot a Tutsi at fifty metres, and vice versa, but to admit to any difference is a taboo subject, even amongst ourselves. The genocide will change the lives of several generations of Rwandans, despite which it is still not mentioned in school textbooks. We have never been comfortable with these nuances which exist between us. In certain ways, ethnicity is like AIDS, the less you dare talk of it, the more ravages it causes.

I have read that after each genocide historians explain that this will be the last. Because no one could again allow such an infamy. That is an amazing joke. Those responsible for the Rwanda genocide are not poor and ignorant farmers, no more than they are ferocious and drunken *interahamwe* – they are the educated people. They are the professors, the politicians and the journalists who expatriated themselves to Europe to study the French revolution and the Humanities. They are those who have travelled, who are invited to conferences and who have invited Whites to eat at their villas. Intellectuals who bought themselves libraries reaching high to the ceiling. Hardly any of them killed with their own hands, but they sent people to the hills to do the job.

In Nyamata, the *interahamwe* president's Christian name was Jean-Désiré. He was a good teacher. Sometimes we would share a Primus together, out of friendship. He would say to us: "Alright, if the *inkotanyi* come into Rwanda, then we will have to kill you," and suchlike. But because he was kind, we laughed about it and offered him another beer. This man, with whom we exchanged jokes, became one of the three or four leading promoters of genocide in the region.

The genocide is not really a question of poverty or a lack of learning, I will explain myself. I am a teacher, so I think that learning is necessary to enlighten us about the world. But it does not make man better, it makes him more efficient. He who wishes to inspire evil will be at an advantage if he knows of man's quirks, if he learns morality, if he studies sociology. If educated man's heart is ill conceived, if he spills over with hatred, he will be more capable of evil-doing. In 1959, the Hutus killed, hunted and looted Tutsis relentlessly, but they did not imagine one day exterminating them. It is the intellectuals who emancipated them, if I may put in this way, inculcating the idea of genocide and freeing them of their reticence. I do not deny the injustices towards Hutus during the reign of the Tutsi kings, the excesses of wealth and authority. But it is such ancient history that so far the national university of Butare has not found a single Rwandan historian capable of writing a suitable book about these matters.

In any case, the Tutsis have committed not a single wickedness since 1959, since after the elections the military became Hutu; the burgomasters, the chiefs of police, policemen, Hutu the same; even the bosses in the post office were Hutu. As for the Tutsis, their herds multiplied, they taught in their classes, built up businesses and grew used to letting themselves be humiliated at traditional times. It is therefore Hutu intellectuals without grievances who planned the removal of the Tutsis.

Furthermore, the French knew that a genocide was in preparation, since they advised our army. They supposedly just did not believe it; nevertheless many Whites knew Habyarimana's programme and his character, as they knew Hitler's. One day, in Nyamata, armoured cars finally came to collect the white Fathers. In the main street, the *interahamwe* believed that they had come to punish them and they fled, yelling at one another that the Whites were to kill them. The tanks did not even stop for a Primus break to have a laugh about the misunderstanding. Also, a few weeks later, the Whites sent professional photographers to show the world how we had been massacred. So you may understand that into the survivors' hearts there slipped a feeling of abandonment that shall never go away. But I do not want to anger you with this.

I see today that there is still embarrassment in talking of the survivors, even amongst Rwandans, even amongst Tutsis. I think that everyone wishes, in certain ways, that the survivors would move aside from genocide. As if they wished to leave to other people, who had not directly run the risk of being cut by machete chops, the task of taking care of it. As if we were now in the way. But it must be said that we are also at fault for this. After the genocide, we were very much asleep, and we lost our heads.

In the forest, a boy had managed to save a radio and batteries. During the first week, in the evening, we heard news of the genocide; we heard the interim Prime Minister's speech, telling off the Hutus of Butare for dragging their feet about hiding the massacre. Later, a speech from the Minister of Agriculture, advising farmers to work with a blade within reach at all times in case a Tutsi runaway passed through their fields. We heard about the disaster in the North, in the South. We said to ourselves that up in our eucalyptus we were amongst the last survivors.

So when we came down, we said to ourselves; "We were meant to die, we are still alive, that is enough for us. What good is there in working or in trying to get by or in getting someone to listen to us?" As for myself, I was destroyed by all this running on Kayumba, I was weakened by malaria, I was dispirited by the death of my family. As if all this misfortune were not enough, my leg blew up on a landmine in the street. I did not seek to rub shoulders with strangers, cameramen and such. I did not care a damn for them, nor for myself, nor for us, nor for what of worth could be said amongst us.

Also, there were some who had stinking wounds too terrible to draw near to, others who found themselves going barefoot, others did not have a roof over their heads. We preferred to stay at home amongst ourselves, we drank Primus the moment we had some pennies. Reporters walked past the door without even knocking, because they were too busy to waste time with people who had nothing more to trade. Tutsis repatriated from Burundi were in much better shape than us, they assumed many activities along the way, they showed more obliging faces, they stood out more.

One thing that surprises me today is that many of the genocide's promoters have become everyday people again, whether they dispersed undisturbed, whether they stroll down streets in France, in Europe, in Kenya. They teach at university, preach in churches or give treatment in hospitals and, in the evening, they listen to music and supervise the children's schooling. It is said: "Genocide is a human folly", but the police will not even question the genocide's leaders in their villas in Brussels or Nairobi. If you ran into one in Paris, with his fashionable suit and his round glasses, you would say, "Well, there's a very civilised African." You would not think: "There is a sadist who stockpiled, then distributed two thousand machetes to peasants from his native hill." So because of this negligence, the killings can begin again, here, or elsewhere.

War is a matter of intelligence and stupidity. A genocide is a matter of the degeneration of intelligence. One thing which is still beyond me, when I speak of this period, is the savagery of the killings. If there were killings to be done, all that had to be done was kill, but why chop arms and legs?

The people who did this are not demons, nor drugged *interahamwe*, as the Whites say. They were neighbouring folk with whom we used to chat on the road to market. There is a place where they skewered five or six Tutsis on a long sharp wooden stick and had them die as kebabs. Now, in the prison at Rilima, they apparently claim that they do not remember how they could have done these incredible things. But they remember everything, down to the smallest detail.

For me – I repeat – they cut and mutilated Tutsis to take from them all that was human and thus kill them more easily. But they made a fundamental mistake. I know of one instance of a killer who buried alive his Tutsi neighbour in a hole behind his house. Eight months later, he heard his victim call to him in a dream. He went into the garden, he removed the earth, he pulled up the corpse, he was arrested. In prison ever since then, he walks day and night, carrying this fellow's skull in a plastic bag. He cannot let go of the bag even to eat. He is haunted in the extreme. Once you have burned children alive, in front of the church at Nyamata, organised hunts for old people in the woods and disembowelled babies from pregnant women in the marshes, you cannot pretend to have forgotten how you could have done this, nor that you were forced to do it.

Furthermore, I think that Rwanda only eats its meagre meal twice daily because of its agriculture; thus many capable arms and hands are needed to stop the bush from getting the upper hand, and that this truth of the land is complementary to the demands of justice.

I notice also that a divide is growing between those who lived through the genocide and other people. An outsider, even though he be Rwandan, even though he be a Tutsi and lost his family during the killings, cannot quite understand the genocide. Even if he saw all those corpses rotting in the bush after the liberation; even if he saw the heaps of corpses in the churches, he cannot share the same vision as us.

Foreigners and returned exiles say that the survivors are becoming bitter, withdrawn, almost aggressive. But this is not true, we are simply a little dispirited because little by little we allowed ourselves to be isolated. We survivors have become more foreign, in this our own land we never left, than all the foreigners and expatriates who look on us with worried eyes.

A Rwandan not directly involved in the genocide thinks that everything a survivor says is true; but that nevertheless he lays it on a bit thick. He believes everything the survivor relates but, an instant later, begins to forget. He acknowledges the thesis of genocide, but he is sceptical as to the details. He who has not lived the genocide wants life to go on as before, wishes to head forward, without too many stops, into the future. To a passing stranger, he offers the following advice: "Alright, it is right to listen to the survivors, but you should also listen to others to fully understand the situation." A Tutsi from outside, who was living in Bujumbura, or in Kampala or in Brussels during the genocide, does not understand these commemorations, these ceremonies of mourning, these memorials. Commemorating all this tires him, he does not want his conscience to relentlessly traumatise him. He does not want to see life in the negative, and that is understandable. To survivors, he advocates: "My friend, stop brooding, try to forget, think of yourself now". There are those who can even say: "At least do it for the people who were killed", or other similar propositions, in order to forget. But the survivor does not want to forget.

Over time, the survivor's memory changes, but not in the same way for everyone. We forget certain details and we mix up other details. We confuse dates and places. Sometimes, someone will tell you that she got machete blows, and the next time she will say it was a blow of a club. It is only a different way of remembering, of telling. On the one hand, we forget things, on the other we learn new information by word of mouth.

On the one hand, we are no longer interested in recounting certain events, on the other hand, we now dare to speak of things we had kept hidden, like being raped, or having abandoned a baby in flight. Faces of friends and family fade, but this does not mean that we neglect them little by little. We forget nothing. For me, I can go several weeks without seeing my late wife and children's faces, though until then I had dreamed of them every night. But never a single day do I forget that they are here no longer, that they were chopped down, that they wanted to exterminate us, that neighbours of long-standing turned in a matter of hours into beasts. Every day, I pronounce the word "genocide".

The survivor cannot stop himself from permanently going back to the genocide. For he who did not experience it, there is a before, a during and an after the genocide, one life with different phases. For us, there is a before, a during and an after too, but these are three distinct lives forever separate. Even though a survivor may show pleasure in resuming his activities and takes a fellow or a neighbouring woman by the hand so as to hurry them up, he knows deep down that he is deluding himself. Even more so for he who speaks of nothing but forgiving and forgetting and reconciliation.

With the survivor, I believe that during the genocide something mysterious locked within the deepest reach of his soul. He knows that he will never know what it is. Therefore he wants to talk of it all the time. There is always something new to say, and to listen to. For instance, someone who was in Kibuye at the time and tells of how it was in Kibuye, and another answers by talking about how it was in Cyangugu, and it could go one forever.

The survivor tends no longer to believe he is really living – that is to say, that he is he who he once was, and in a certain way, he lives on this a little.

8

A shop on the main street

In Nyamata, the friendliest *cabaret* isn't a *cabaret*. It's Marie-Louise's shop opposite the market. It can be found by its wall inscription: "Prudence" and adjoins a real *cabaret*, La Fraternité, which, despite the charm of its patio, its exotic frescoes, its starry ceiling, is as deserted as the other cafés in town. Marie-Louise's shop, on the other contrary, confined within faded green walls, lit by a single neon lamp in the evening, is always packed.

At the back of the room hang cuts of magnificent Rwandan fabric in a range of blue and striped fabric from the Congo. On the shelves, Thermos flasks, bags, underwear, sachets of rice, copy-books, padlocks... A high counter with a glass display exhibits ballpoint pens, batteries, shampoos. A refrigerator thrums against the wall. In the drowsy afternoon hours, the mistress of the premises sits on a bench outside, gazing dreamily at the square, and in the evening, in a comfortable armchair behind the counter. She has a welcoming face. She is dressed with traditional Rwandan elegance, speaks in a suave drawl.

Behind the shop door, a sofa, a bench, some stools, surround a low table. From the midday break to late at night, this place is never bereft of drinkers. A circle of local intellectuals, as well as those from Kayumba, shopkeepers and high street regulars, all meet here. Here you find the most faithful of the faithful, who couldn't imagine a day going by without dropping in for a drink: Innocent, of course; Sylvère and Gonzalve, two school directors;

Benoît, a cattle breeder, shod in boots and wearing a western-style felt hat; André, the very discreet and poker-faced first deputy; Titi, star of a great football team which went up into the first division, now a coach... Jean, Marie-Louise's right-hand man and tireless chauffeur, must be added to the list, as well as the hilarious Englebert who, if he didn't exist, would have to be invented. Son of a great family – royalty, he sometimes proclaims on his third beer – erudite, high-ranking civil servant and polyglot when sober, Englebert, fearing the massacres, fled the capital and came to the marshes. Since then, no one and nothing can persuade him to return to the town and to his office. He lives half the time as a hermit in a hovel lost in the woods. When he's not helping someone out with the drafting of a little task, paid for with a Primus, he spends the rest of his time between Marie-Louise's boutique – on prosperous days – or in *urwagwa* joints, looking desperately for a past which is receding, quoting Shakespeare and Baudelaire, playing, not without humour, the role of group joker or village idiot.

Marie-Louise knows each one's habits: lukewarm Primus for Innocent, cool Amstel for Sylvère, a large Mutzig for Dominique, a little Mutzig for Benoît... She replaces empty bottles while at the same time serving regular shoppers, or pampering an impoverished child. Sipping a Coca-Cola, she gets involved in discussions. At her shop, you comment on the news on the radio, the latest town gossip, and joke a lot. Beer after beer, you end by telling stories about the genocide, you recollect memories of memories, you laugh about a feat or a disaster. Complicity, an often black humour, an impressive mutual tolerance, help maintain an atmosphere which its regulars can no longer do without. Marie-Louise's boutique is also a place where you have a drink after a funeral or a baptism, where you can leave a message.

Why Marie-Louise's and not La Fraternité? Or the magnificent and permanently deserted garden at L'Intzinsi, or the Podium even, so many places which were once jumping. The first answer has to do with a response from the period immediately after the genocide. At the time, the town looked as though devastated by a hurricane. The survivors were coping with poverty, while exiles returning from Burundi had yet to find their bearings and were wary of this depopulated and traumatised town. Hutus returning from the Congo didn't dare go into the town centre, fearing reprisal or denunciation and so kept to themselves in the hills. The *cabarets* remained silent, the abandoned terrasses all too clearly underlined the number of people absent, whether dead or in prison. Drinkers instinctively preferred to gather in shops, in drink warehouses, workshops, places more intimate, less haunted, where beer is a little less expensive. In this way many found themselves at Marie-Louise's, married once upon a time to the region's wealthiest shipper.

This initial reaction has become a custom. L'Intzinsi and the bar at the cultural centre, formerly frequented by the extremists, are abandoned, despite new owners. The Podium hasn't reopened. Le Club or La Fraternité don't "jump" anymore. Only the mournful *bistrots* in remote alleys, which offer a bitter banana wine at very modest prices, have found again their faithful clientele.

The second reason for the success of Marie-Louise's shop is of course due to its owner's graciousness: her perpetual smile, her devotion to her guests, her discretion when she wipes the slate clean for the most hard-up, when she sends home a drowsy drinker or cools down an argument. As Innocent has nicely put it: not enough superlatives survived the genocide to describe the kindness of Marie-Louise, whom no one would now dare forsake.

Marie Louise Kagoyire
45 years old, shopkeeper
Nyamata High Street

My parents were small farmers and cattle breeders. They gave me permission to finish my first year in secondary school before I had to leave in search of a husband. With us, girls would marry earlier when their parents were not rich.

One day I came to Nyamata to visit a maternal aunt. On the main square, a man spotted me and liked me well. His name was Léonard Rwerekana, he was already a well-known shopkeeper. We began by exchanging the odd wink. In those days, though, a young girl was strictly forbidden to agree directly to anything at all. He therefore asked my aunt to act as go-between. My aunt persevered with my family; and the man walked a whole day in the sun to go and see my parents; they said that a man who has walked so far should not be made any more tired. I married at the age of nineteen.

At that time, Nyamata was a small town of mud brick houses with sheet metal roofs. It was only in 1974 that the first solid houses were built. Léonard built his first house on our plot, then a warehouse in the high street, then new shops. In 1976, he bought a van; it was very clapped out, but it was the first private vehicle. Then he opened a *cabaret*, La Fraternité, some restaurants, built up a business in beans and drinks, he bought land and cows. In 1980, he had two new vans up and running, he was the biggest shipper in the region. There were already incipient jealousies between Tutsi and Hutu shopkeepers because the Tutsis were doing better than the Hutus. One of the reasons for this is that the latter came from Gitarama and had no knowledge of the Nyamata clientele. Another reason is that Tutsis keep their hired hands for five or six years, until they themselves may open their own small business, contrary to Hutus who never stop changing them.

Most important, however, is that Tutsis own their stock and never borrow money from anyone.

On the day the plane crashed, the Tutsis who lived in the town centre could no longer go out. Many people came seeking protection behind the solid brick wall around our house. Léonard had known several massacres in his youth and understood that the situation this time was catastrophic and advised young people to make tracks to Kayumba. But he himself did not want to flee, he said that his legs had already done enough running.

On the morning of the 11th of April, the first day of the massacres, the *interahamwe* turned up in a great uproar right in front of our gate. Léonard took the keys and went to open up without delay, thinking that in this way he could save the women and children. A soldier shot him dead without uttering one word. A mass of *interahamwe* came into the courtyard, they caught all the children they could, they laid them in rows on the ground, they began to cut them. They even killed a Hutu boy, the son of a colonel who was there with his friends. As for me, I managed to skirt around the house with my mother-in-law and we lay down behind piles of tyres. The killers stopped before the end, because they were in a great hurry to start looting. We could hear them. They got into our cars, our vans, they loaded them with crates of Primus, they argued over furniture and all sorts of things; they searched under the beds for money.

That evening, my mother-in-law came out of the hiding place and sat down in front of the tyres. Some young people noticed and asked her: "Maman, what are you doing here?" She answered: "I no longer do anything, because now I am alone." They took her, they chopped her, then they took what was left in the bedrooms and the living room. They lit a fire; this is how they forgot me.

In the courtyard there was a child who had not been killed. So I put a ladder up against the dividing wall, I climbed up with the child and jumped into our neighbour Florient's place. His

courtyard was empty. I hid the child in the log storeroom and I huddled up in the dog's kennel. On the third morning, I heard the sound of footsteps and I spotted my neighbour, I came out. My neighbour exclaimed: "Marie-Louise, they are killing everyone in town, your house has been burned, but you are still here? Now, what can I do for you?" I said to him: "Florient, do this for me – kill me. But do not expose me to the *interahamwe* who will undress and chop me."

Monsieur Florient was a Hutu. He was head of military intelligence in the Bugesera, but had built his house on our plot and, before the war, we would speak to one another kindly, share good moments, our children ran around together in the courtyards. So he locked myself and the child up in his home, he gave us some food to eat and he went away. The next day he warned me: "Marie-Louise, they are checking corpses in town and have not found your face. They are looking for you. You must leave, because if they find you here in my home, then they will fine me with my life."

That night, he took us to a Hutu acquaintance of his who was hiding a small number of Tutsi acquaintances. One day, the *interahamwe* came knocking on the door to search the house. The lady of the house went out to talk to them, she returned, and she said: "Has anyone got any money on them?" I gave her a wad of notes I carried in my cloth. She kept a small amount for herself, she went back out to the *interahamwe*, who left. Every day, the bargaining began again, and the woman was becoming very nervous. One day, Monsieur Florient warned me: "Marie-Louise, the young men in town hold too great a grudge against you, you must leave." I repeated to him: "Florient, you have the materials, kill me, I want to die in a house. Do not abandon me in the hands of the *interahamwe*." He said: "I am not going to kill my wife's friend. If I found transport, would you have the money to pay for it?" I gave him another wad of notes, he counted them out and said: "That is quite something, sure to be enough." He came back and suggested: "We will put you in a sack and take you into the forest, then you will have to fend for yourself." At the same time he asked: "The *interahamwe* have looted your house, the soldiers will leave with money. Is it right that I who have saved you will have nothing to show for it?" So I said to him: "Florient, I have two villas in Kigali, take them. The shop in the high street, I leave it to you. I will sign a paper granting you power of attorney over everything. But I want you to accompany me to Burundi."

We left – me lying down in an army van between the driver and Florient. I first stayed in his house at the military base at Gako. I was locked up in a bedroom. When everyone was asleep, someone brought me food. I only had a cloth on me. This lasted weeks, I do not know how long anymore. One night, a friend of Florient's came in. He explained: "The *inkotanyi* are coming at speed, we are going to evacuate the barracks. It's too awkward to keep you here, I have to take you away." He put me aboard a truck which delivered sacks to the front. We drove – all road blocks opened up for us – we entered a dark forest, the driver stopped beneath the trees. I shivered and said to him: "Alright, I have nothing left. It is my turn to die now. As long as it is fast." He answered: "Marie-Louise, I am not going to kill you here, because I work for Florient. Go straight as a die, and never stop. When the forest comes to an end, you will lay your hand on the Burundi frontier-post and on deliverance." I walked, I fell, I crawled on my hands and knees. When I came to the frontier-post, I heard voices calling out in the dark, I fell asleep.

Later, a Burundian associate of my husband came in a van to collect me from the refugee camp. When he looked at me, he did not recognise me. He did not even want to believe I was Léonard's wife. I had lost twenty kilos, I was wearing a cloth made out of sacking, I had swollen feet, a head full of lice. Monsieur Florient now awaits trial at the prison in Rilima. He was an officer. He left every morning and every evening came back with tales of the killings in town. In the corridor I saw

91

piles of new axes and machetes. He spent my money, he looted my wares. Despite this, never will I go to court to accuse him, because, when all anyone could think of was killing, he saved one life.

I returned to Nyamata at the end of the genocide in July. Not a single member of my family in Mugesera had survived, not a single member of my family in Nyamata either, the neighbouring folk were dead, the warehouse looted, the trucks stolen. I had lost everything, I was indifferent to life. Nyamata was very desolate, since all the roofs, all the doors and windows, had been taken off. But it was above all time itself that seemed broken in the town. It seemed as though it had stopped forever or, on the contrary, had flown all too quickly in our absence. I mean that we no longer knew when it had all begun, the number of days and nights it had lasted, what season it was, and truly in the end we didn't care. The children went out to catch hens in the undergrowth; we started to eat meat, we began to fix things, we tried to get back into at least some of the old routines. We took one day at a time, which we spent seeking the company of friends with whom we could spend the night, so as to avoid running the risk of dying, forsaken in a nightmare.

One morning, some friends came to me with a sum of money and said: "Marie-Louise, take this. You know how to bargain, not us; you must start your business again." I had the shop door put back on; the trade came back, but all hope had gone. Before, prosperity held its arms out to me. Léonard and I went from one task to the next, we were happy, we were liked and respected. Now I look at life, all of it, in a dire way, I keep an eye out for dangers great and small everywhere. I no longer have the one who loved me, I can no longer find a shoulder to lean on.

At the shop, clients tell me about how they survived. In the evening, I listen to acquaintances discuss the massacres. And still I understand nothing about anything. With the Hutus, we shared things, we backed one another financially, we married, and there they go all of sudden hunting us like wild animals. I do not believe that envy is the explanation, because out of envy no one crushes children to death, lined up in rows in a courtyard, with blows from a club. I do not believe in this story of beauty or feelings of inferiority. In the hills, Tutsi and Hutu women alike were muddy and damaged by work in the fields; in the towns, both Hutu and Tutsi children alike were beautiful and smiling.

The Hutus had the luck to monopolise all state favours and promotions for themselves, they obtained good harvests because they farmed well, they opened profitable businesses, in retail at least. We shook hands on deals in a friendly fashion, we lent them money; and they decided to cut us to pieces. So great was their desire to wipe us out that they were obsessive enough to burn our photo albums as they looted, so that not even the dead would have the chance of having once existed. For greater security, they wanted to kill not just people but their memories too, and in any case, kill the memories when they could not catch the people. They worked hard at our extinction and on extinguishing all traces of their work, if I may put it like this. Today, many survivors have not even one tiny photo of their maman, of their children, of their baptisms and marriages, they do not have an image which could spread a little balm over their regrets.

As for me, I can see that the sole reason for this genocidal hatred lies in ethnic belonging. In nothing else, like feelings of fear, frustration, or whatever. But the origin of this hatred is still well concealed for me. The why of this hatred, the why of the genocide – you cannot ask survivors, it is too difficult a question for them to answer. It is even too delicate. You must let them talk about it amongst themselves. You must ask the Hutus.

Sometimes, Hutu women come back to me asking for work on the plots. I talk to them, try to ask them why they wanted to kill us without ever having complained of anything before. But they do not want to know about it. They keep saying that they did nothing, that they saw nothing, that their husbands were not *interahamwe*, that it is the authorities who are at fault for what happened. They say it was the *interahamwe* who forced neighbours to cut, otherwise they would have been themselves killed, and they seem happy enough with this for an answer. I say to myself: "These Hutus killed without hesitation and now they avoid discussions about the truth. This is not acceptable." Which is why I am not sure it will not start all over again some day.

Everyone came out of the genocide a great loser: Tutsis, Hutus, the survivors, the *interahamwe*, shopkeepers, farmers, families, children, all Rwandans. Perhaps even foreigners and Whites who did not want to see what was happening and who felt a belated pity.

Furthermore, I think that foreigners tend to show all too comparable pity towards people who have suffered misfortunes not at all comparable, as if the pity were more important than the misfortune. I also believe that should any foreigner take a close look at what we suffered during the genocide, they shall never get beyond that pity. It is perhaps for this reason that they look at us from a distance. But it seems all in the past.

More important is that life fell to pieces here, that wealth went off, that no one pays attention to his neighbour, that people become sad and nasty over nothing at all, that people no longer rate kindness as before, that men are broken, that women have lost heart. All this is very worrisome.

Amongst ourselves, we never grow tired of talking about this post-genocide state of things. We talk to one another about the moments we went through, we swap explanations, we tease one another and, if someone gets angry, we gently joke with him to bring him back to us. But to show our hearts to a stranger, to speak of what we feel, to lay bare our survivors' sentiments, this is too shocking. When an exchange of words becomes too blunt, as now with you, then it is time to come to a full stop.

9

The penitentiary of Rilima

A thin cord strung tight between two acacias, watched over by a guard sitting astride a chair, marks the entrance to the prison at Rilima. Don't be taken in by such casualness – no aspiring escapee has ever got beyond this forest, nor from nearby Lake Kidogo.

Formerly the central prison, the penitentiary today now incarcerates more than eight thousand prisoners, suspected or convicted of having taken part in the genocide in the Bugesera region, primarily in the commune of Nyamata. Guard and administrative shacks are lined up in the shade. On a track leading down to the lake goes an unending procession of jerry can bearers in pink uniforms, carrying out water chores. By the shore, the privileged clean themselves, or do their laundry.

Without watchtower or barbed wire, the wall of the prison house itself stands out on a rise. A half-open orange iron gate lets out authorized prisoners. Fifty metres from this gate you are struck both by the din of musicians and singers hurling competing rhythms and chants at each other, and by the overpowering smell of sweat, and no doubt also of food and rubbish. One look through the opening gives you an inkling as to the indescribable overcrowding which reigns within these walls. Three buildings house male prisoners, a fourth houses female. But because the prison population here has multiplied tenfold since the penitentiary was put to its latest use, prisoners live where they can. Some are crammed into shacks and cells. Most are packed into the courtyard, whether squatting shoulder to shoulder in the sun, or sheltering beneath metal and plastic sheeting. It's in the midst of this crush that the prisoners, all dressed in pink uniforms, cook their meals in giant cauldrons, hang up washing, beat drums, organize political and prayer meetings under the auspices of former chiefs, political personalities, or priests. It's in this scrum that the hard-headed fight for space in which to weave, to build, play cards or checkers, bet and sometimes fight, sleep or pass the time. You see faces solemn and sad, perhaps desperate and filled with hate; others are fatalist, jovial, polite.

Though none can escape the overcrowding – aggravated by heat wave and rain showers – the prisoners are subject to different disciplinary regulations. Those who have confessed – more than two thousand – as well as those who are suspected of secondary misdemeanours – are contained in a separate building and can move around more freely. They do gardening work near the administrative buildings, fix cars, play football on a pitch outside the grounds, talk under the trees. Most of those awaiting trial hang about in the courtyard. At dawn some are trucked to work on the seventy-two hectares of fields that belong to the prison. Those condemned to death or to long prison sentences wait behind bars. They describe the prison as a "hell on earth", to use one of their expressions.

Like all the prisons which incarcerate killers of the genocide, Rilima is subject to a dual authority: that of the guards, absent from the prison courtyard, who control the periphery; that of the local mafia, former *interahamwe* chiefs or unrepentant ideologues from the genocide, who have re-established inside a hierarchy reflecting militia and extremist party affiliation. They control the buildings, organize training and festivities, supervise gifts, settle disputes, brief defendants before their trial.

Without prior permission from the court or the prison administration, prisoners' parents are allowed to visit for two or three minutes. They come in waves of two or three hundred, leave food and clothes, exchange a few words and leave. The International Red Cross inspects the whole prison area. In exchange, it provides, for a limited period, the bulk of supplies (jerry cans, basins, mattresses), medicine and food, without which this penitentiary would become "hell on earth" for all prisoners.

Strangely, the Hutus, whether villagers or city people, whether they confess to their crimes or deny them, whether they feel guilty or not, talk almost more freely here in the prison about the killings than they do at home. Doubtlessly because they no longer feel safe in the hills, running the risk of denunciation or sometimes arbitrary arrest. In the Nyamata territory, two out of three inhabitants of Hutu origin have gone back to their land. Those still absent, especially men, unless they are at prison in Rilima, were either killed during the war or haven't returned from the Congo, or have chosen to return to the village of their birth, far from the gaze of neighbours who survived.

Aside from the schools, where all children sit together on the same benches, aside from the market, because it can't be otherwise, aside from the church on Sunday or the occasional funeral wake, Hutus and Tutsis now avoid each other. On the hills, Hutu families give strangers a hospitable welcome full of kindness, yet also timid and anxious. The moment the genocide is brought up during conversation, silence falls like a shroud over their memories, including those of Hutus cleared by the testimony of a Tutsi neighbour.

One day, on the hill of Maranyundo, living on a slope inhabited by Hutu families, a young woman encountered by chance, breaks this silence. Indeed, she proves to be confident and talkative. She agrees to talk about her family, her Hutu village, her youth, her life as a farmer. Then, curiously, as the genocide is raised, she doesn't tense up or try to change the subject. On the contrary, without hesitation she retraces the events with all the detachment of a spectator still shocked by what she has seen, describes her neighbours' reactions, tells of her fear of *interahamwe*, then of her rash flight, the Hutu horde's great exodus, the long trek through a country at war, the camps in the Congo, the return, her future.

Her name is Christine Nyiransabimana. With her mother and her two brothers, she works the family plot. She is the single mother of a boy, who, though an unwanted pregnancy, is nevertheless pampered, as she explains herself, and of two very much wanted twin girls. A frank and a very friendly smile lights up her face. She knows plenty about her own people. During the first visit, without going into detail, she barely alludes to her father's murder. It's only during the second visit that she reveals, with an enigmatic reticence, why he was killed.

Christine Nyiransabimana
22 years old, farmer
Hill of Maranyundo

I came to the region in 1980, in the midst of migrations of Hutu compatriots, because my parents were getting thin on an all too crusty plot of land in Kibuye. Many Tutsis were already claiming the Bugesera for themselves, but brand new plots were still being distributed to Hutus.

At the beginning of the war, I was in the fifth year of primary. At this time, we saw on the hill more and more young men with malicious faces, not all from the region. They entered Hutu houses without saying their names and stuffed themselves from our pots. When these *interahamwe* attacked the church at Nyamata, a small crowd formed and watched the killing. We could hear the noise of blows, cries of encouragement, we listened to the fear of those about to be chopped; you saw young men pushing each other around to steal the goods of those killed or loot the abbots' rooms.

We saw bulldozers bury the unfortunate like rubbish, in a large hole. Some were saying that not everyone was dead, but it seemed that the criminals' objective was to have the burials over and done with that afternoon. In the evening, they went off to eat, but the church remained surrounded by vigilant look-outs. Inside, the people waited all night; those who would die of their wounds waited for death.

The *interahamwe* returned at around nine in the morning and began again to hit and skewer those people who continued to live. It was a sort of show lasting two days. Many spectators were content to see Tutsis dying, they cried: "The Tutsis, they are finished! Get rid of these cockroaches for us!" But I should also say that a great number of people were very indignant to see them killed and burned so wickedly. But it was very dangerous to utter more than a murmur of protest, for without hesitation the *interahamwe* killed those Hutus on good terms with Tutsis in their neighbourhood. That too is the truth: in the crowd around the church, those people who were not excited were very frightened.

On the second evening, some *interahamwe* returning from the church turned up at our house, and they chopped Papa with a machete, in front of Maman and neighbours. Papa was called François Sayinzoga, he was Tutsi.

In my area, and in Nyamata town, I saw many Hutu relations and neighbours killing Tutsis every day of the genocide, following the *interahamwe* or the soldiers. On the road in the evening, these farmers swapped boasts about their work in the marshes or in the forests. They sat on chairs in front of their dwellings; the women prepared meat since they were slaughtering cows at the same time as Tutsis. They bought drink for themselves, because they had taken money off the dead. And on a full stomach, they talked of their day, this is to say – how many people they had killed. They held contests. Some would say they had killed two, others ten. Those who had not killed pretended that they had, so as not to be threatened in turn. I can say that it was everyone's duty to kill. It was a very well organized plan.

Every morning, people had to report to their group chief. In Maranyundo, the chief, whose first name was Vincent, demanded to be called Goliath. It was from him that people got their orders and itineraries for the day. Either they went along, or else they would be killed. They could pretend to drag their feet at the back of the group and return in the evening without having dirtied their machetes, but they had to show up. Those who marched without doing anything during the day could not loot anything. Those who claimed they had too much furrowed earth to sow on their land and who tried to come up with excuses could be shot in passing.

Which is also the reason why the farmers did not bury their victims. When they named the Tutsis they had cut down that day, and if they were suspected of cheating, they had to take the *interahamwe* and show them the corpses. I believe that he who was obliged to kill one day wanted his neighbour to be obliged to do so the next, so as to be in the same boat.

As for us, we felt guilty for living in the midst of this blood lust; and we were truly very frightened by Papa's death. So we continued to scratch the fields in silence.

Men began discussing massacres in the *cabarets* in 1992. After the first party meetings *interahamwe* committees sprang up in the communes, and the chemistry was no longer good between us. The leader in the commune of Nyamata went by the first name of Joseph-Désiré. He travelled from one Hutu dwelling to the next, elaborating on the threats coming from *inkotanyi* in Uganda, he checked that the tools behind the bean sacks were well sharpened. When Hutus shared a drink together after political discussions, they called the Tutsis "worms" or, in the same vein, "cockroaches". The radios were becoming very menacing. At home, Papa and my brothers did not get mixed up in chat which could spark off contempt,

because they were wary of poisonous glances. We avoided the *interahamwe*, we made do with seeing only our nearest neighbours with whom we had always rubbed shoulders. We drew water together, we gave each other a light, we sometimes shared a beer together, we never exchanged political words.

In the region, you lived according to order of arrival. Those who had come in such and such a year took one hill; those who followed went to the hill behind. This did not make for easy ethnic mixing. When you do not mix with one another, you do not appreciate each other enough to marry. This is why we never went asking after marriage to a Tutsi. As for Papa and Maman, they had met in Kibuye, before travelling out here.

This is another truth of importance: the *interahamwe* wanted to kill all Tutsis married to Hutus, and even peaceful Hutus linked with Tutsis. After Papa's death, neighbouring folk hurled threats at me because I had Tutsi blood. So as not to be killed I considered myself Hutu, but I was frightened. So I fled with a Hutu to Kigali, leaving Maman and my brothers behind in the house. At the end of the great rains, as RPF rifles began to crackle in the outskirts of Kigali, we felt the war laying a hand upon us. *Interahamwe* killers came to loot the house, they took away all the utensils and furniture in their stampede. These evil-doers, who had drunk beer, forced me onto the bed and left me with a baby in the belly. It was in May, as I remember. A great disorder was spreading everywhere. Runaways were robbing from all sides; they screamed death and panic. All this frantic racing around heated the spirits. So I put on two sets of clothes, one over the other, and a sweater, and without thinking I rushed out and joined the fleeing scrum. We walked for at least six weeks, without stopping, because of all the alarming rumours.

All along the road as we went, it was said that a deadly danger was hot on our heels and must not catch up with us. Those who had money hidden got on trucks, the penniless walked. We were at the end of our tether, our legs and feet swelled up, the weakest let themselves drop by the wayside and died, the others walked on because of the evil pronouncements being made. It was often repeated that Ugandan soldiers would revenge their Rwandan brothers and that bad luck had switched camp. We ate bananas and manioc we had stolen from the fields, we tried to heat up a soup made of leaves. We slept on the ground. We were quite simply enveloped in fear and shame.

Everywhere the chaos was the same. In June, we put in for a long stopover in Gisenyi, then we beat a retreat towards the Congo. Many Whites came to the roadside to watch us as we went. We were fugitives, we had come in for a very rough ride, and this was good enough for them. I was sent to the camp in Mugunga, some ten kilometres from Goma, where I lasted two years.

In the camp, some of us went gathering wood, others cooked rice balls; those who had kept their savings did business. As for me, I went on foot to Goma to do laundry in Congolese people's dwellings or scratch the earth in gardens and collected bananas and manioc by way of reward. In the beginning, the Congolese looked tenderly upon us, but little by little they hardened. Life became very forlorn.

I gave birth alone, in an alien tent, without one old maman to hold my hand, without one acquaintance to prepare gruel. With the baby, I remained in good health, but I ate pitifully. I was too unhappy about what was going on. In the evening, by the fire, I suffered a great longing for the family plot in Maranyundo. I longed to return, but the *interahamwe* spread threats around the camp. All the time we believed we would be assailed from every direction because of the evil the *interahamwe* and the soldiers had done.

In November 1997, the *banyamulinge* guns drove us out of the camp. Tutsis from the Congo are called *banyamulinge*. It was early morning in the fog; a great stampede followed. I walked for days following a group through the mountains of Masisi.

We fled, bogged down in fear, without knowing one another and without knowing our way. Guns raised, the *banyamulinge* encircled our group. A soldier persuaded me peace lay waiting for me in Rwanda, since I had not killed, and that I would find again the harmony of the old days in my home and in the fields.

So I went walking in the opposite direction, in the company of a traveller I met by chance. On the road home, no one spoke to anyone, I crossed the country without a word. I was questioned at the village. When I saw Maman and my brother alive, I finally felt my first hope. They had been back for a very long time, since they had not got as far into the Congo. With great joy, they took me back to the house.

Nothing had taken the place of death in the abandoned plots. I was greatly ashamed to be regarded as a Hutu, as if I were like the people who had massacred so much. Even today, the same dream catches me in my sleep. We are in flight to the Congo, we are crossing a field covered in corpses, to the north of Kigali, I step over corpses, but still they keep turning up before me, I keep stepping over more corpses, and it never stops, I cannot stop walking over corpses and am unable to leave the field. Then I wake up and speak to Maman, she speaks to me without waking up the children. We conjure up the troubles each of us went through, then a comforting sleep takes us.

In the beginning when I went to market, I encountered hard gazes and heard rebukes as I passed – from Tutsi women mourning for their families and Hutu women who feared that their husbands' misdeeds would be denounced. Little by little they faded, but we still are esteemed very lowly and I suffer from it greatly. I even feel worried for this, for many Hutu women dipped their hands in the blood of the genocide. Men are more inclined to kill and to be reconciled than women. They forget more quickly, they share killings and drink more easily. Women do not forget in the same way, they hold on to more memories.

But I also know good women, Hutus, who do not dare offer

compassion after what their neighbours had done, for fear of being accused in turn. I know that life can no longer be calm as it once was; nevertheless, when the food is good, when the children sleep well, when we feel at rest, we forget melancholy for a little while.

There is war when authorities want to overthrow other authorities and help themselves in their stead. A genocide is one ethnic group that wants to bury another ethnic group. A genocide surpasses war, because the intention endures forever, even if it is not crowned with success. In Rwanda, there were only two ethnic groups. The Hutus therefore thought it would be more convenient to remain alone cultivating the fields and doing deals. They saw a more comfortable future amongst themselves. I believe that ignorance and greed are at the origin of the disaster. It's not just the Whites who taught envy and fear of Tutsis to Hutus, it was President Habyarimana and his wife Agathe too, who never tired of riches.

In Rwanda, we are all black in the same manner, we eat red beans of the same seed, sorghum in the same season, we sing hymns together in the churches. The Hutus and the Tutsis are not very different. Nevertheless, a Hutu can easily recognise a Tutsi, if he wants to find him. You begin with the height, though you may have it wrong, for the Tutsi is no longer as tall as before. So you look at the face. A Tutsi's expression is a polite one, in a certain way his words are softer. Even when he digs a plot of misery, his stomach hollow, his garments in tatters, the Tutsi always feels more bourgeois, because he is descended from an ethnic group that raised cattle. Tutsis often have a stiff posture, if I may say so, when they walk and even when they greet one another. They like to go along with a stick.

The Hutu does not understand cows, he does not like to go to any great effort over cows. He does not celebrate festivities in the same way. The Hutu likes to work, eat well, and enjoy himself. If not pushed, the Hutu does not think of evil. He very quickly feels at his ease. He is more easy-going or rustic, in some ways more cheerful, more joyful. He is more at ease with things and less anxious about difficulties. He is neither wicked nor rancorous by nature.

The truth is that the Hutus loved their president too much. When he died, they did not take the time to gather for a drink; to talk, to cry, to wake and to mourn together in our Rwandan manner. It was a very serious shortcoming to immediately go out onto the roads yelling threats. Too many radios were shaking spirits up, as I have told you, too many big men inflaming little people. It had been prepared for a long time. Therefore, at the signal, farmers started killing and stealing, and they developed a taste for these new activities.

But I repeat that they were obliged. If they tried to come up with excuses or pretexts for working without getting mixed up with anything, neighbours could easily have killed them on their land. On the hill, I know many a Hutu who never cut, but none that never took part in the chase, except those who fled like the Tutsis.

I know Hutus who acknowledge their mistakes and who agree to being punished. Hutus who deny everything and think that all traces of their killings will be lost. Others truly believe that they did not kill, even though people saw them, a red blade in the hand; they have gone mad from their madness. Others cannot evaluate what they did, as if they just did something silly in secret and that is all. One day, Maman went to the trial of one of Papa's killers, a neighbour. He meets Maman in the courthouse corridor, says kindly good morning to her, he asks for news of the family, the rains, the plot, then he says goodbye and goes back to prison as if he were going home. Maman stood there gobsmacked before starting to weep.

It is now impossible to draw a line of truth through what we have done. All I see is that evil fell upon us and we held out our arms to it. Now, I live by the hoe from Monday to Saturday. On Sundays I rest and feel nostalgia for former times. I see that I have not married because of all of this. I regret this very much. I have gathered children on the way, as I have explained to you. I no longer have any problems with the neighbours. We sell each other some goods, we bid one another good morning, that is all. I hope that time will lend us a hand in cleaning away the stains. If Hutus tried to tell the truth out loud, to offer mutual help, to go to the Tutsis and ask for pardon, then we could hope to live well together, without being forever separated by what happened.

10

A secret flight

The sudden din of a flock of stunning soui-mangas –
green backs, blue bellies – and red grosbeaks – black
with scarlet throats – parachuting into the banana groves, brings
conversation to an end. In front of Christine's house, a path
enters a forest of trees flowering in red, and crosses over a
muddy river on two worm-eaten tree trunks. Here and there,
behind the thick foliage, you can make out round huts inhabited
by Twa pygmies – rarely ever met. From Christine's to Odette
Mukamusoni's former home, it's a short distance.

Odette and Christine, born a year apart on adjacent hills, are
both farmers and mothers to children of the same age. Since
childhood, they have met on the paths leading to the school and
the wells, but they have never addressed a single word to each
other, despite the fact that now, more than ever, they would have
much in the way of memories and insights to exchange,
especially on their respective escapes during the massacres.

Odette has recently left the hill to live in a shack on the
outskirts of Nyamata. Her family perished during the killings.
The father of her child went into exile in the Congo. The ruins of
her house has vanished beneath creeping vegetation, the bush
has invaded the fields. So many reasons to explain why she
refuses to start life again in her village. Innocent Rwililiza met
her by chance, near the church, in the midst of a group of
volunteer workers who were digging up bones from the mass
grave to store them away out of the rains. Odette was working

by herself, seemed lost-looking and shocked by what she had been through, which she retold him that day. At the time, far from home, her isolation didn't come as a surprise to him. He found her a temporary home in a little straw hut.

During the first meeting, Odette tells of how she fled to the church when the killings began, of her miraculous survival in a Brazilian nun's bedroom, how at a friend of her godmother's she hid under the bed. In minute detail, she recounts how she stayed there a month, hidden under the bed during the day, the agony of listening to the killers chatting in the house, the waiting, the boredom, the solitude, the latent depression, the rescue. She weaves details together, which, however extraordinary, are still plausible. Nevertheless, something odd arouses my suspicion. It's not so much how outlandish the story of her survival is, nor her actual loneliness – the fate of many traumatized survivors – it's more her chronological exactitude, her accumulation of details... to put it briefly, an accuracy of memory too good to be true.

As of the second meeting, Odette gives up defending the first version. She admits her invention, which she justifies by her fear of being misunderstood by her neighbours. Relieved, she then spontaneously offers to relate as follows the true version, just as surprising as the first. One episode in her escape, too sensitive to have been made public because it would inevitably have given rise to rumours and suspicions, explains her initial lie, explains her fear and her leaving the hill where she was born.

Odette Mukamusoni

23 years old, mason's mate
Hill of Kanazi

My father owned eight cows, but he withdrew me from primary school because I was his fourth daughter. Pre-war, I was thus an employee, indoors and outdoors, for cleaning or for chores in the fields.

In the region, there had always been killings and house burnings, but each time we said to ourselves they would turn out no worse than usual. The atmosphere changed in 1994. At the time of the first rains, we grew alarmed about war because neighbouring Hutu folk no longer exchanged greetings with us on the road. They yelled threats instead, they repeated: "Tutsis who see far should walk far, because soon every nearby Tutsi will be dead." At home, in the evenings, we furtively talked about it. But my father refused to leave the hill, because he could not envisage a future for himself without his cows. As for me, I found a quiet job in our capital, Kigali.

When the plane dropped, I was a *boyeste* in Nyakabanda, a good neighbourhood in Kigali. The mistress of the household, whose Christian name was Gloria, was Tutsi. Her husband, Joseph, was a very kind Hutu merchant. One day of the genocide, the *interahamwe* opened the living-room door. The husband was away on a business trip in Kenya; his brother was unable to save the lady's life. The *interahamwe* killed the family on the carpet. I was hiding on my belly in a box room. They did not search the house, because they had simply wished to get rid of the lady and her children in the husband's absence, and so they were satisfied.

An hour later, looters entered and surprised me in the house. They were preparing to cut me up on the spot when one of them, who answered to the first name of Callixte, protected me from his fellows. He was carrying a gun, he was the chief. He took me for his wife because he no longer had one. At his home, I heard through the doors that the killing programme was on schedule everywhere and that by the dry season there would not be a single Tutsi child left standing. So I said to myself that since God has so far authorized me to keep my life in hiding, then I should not waste it. Which is the reason why I never attempted to escape and run the risk of dying amongst other Tutsis.

I lived in Callixte's dwelling until the arrival of the *inkotanyi*

in July. After this, he took me away on the distressing flight to
the Congo, of which you have heard much news. We lived first
in Gisenyi, under the protection of the French soldiers, with
some of Callixte's family. Then we travelled on to the Congo.
We spent a year and a half in the camp at Mugunga. I was very
confused by all the macabre rumours, and no longer expected
anything from life. We lived in a tent. I was a wife for Callixte,
who was never bad to me. The camp co-inhabitants knew I was
Tutsi. They never dared say anything in front of Callixte,
because he was an *interahamwe* of great importance, but when
he went away on rounds of meetings, I heard malicious and
upsetting gossip ring out. On a November day in 1996, I
approached a gathering of white trucks belonging to a humanitarian organization. Whites were saying that whoever wanted to
return to Rwanda had only to get aboard, it was free. Callixte
had gone away on an expedition, I climbed up onto the skip
along with a great many others. The truck drove as far as the
border. New white trucks were waiting for us the other side of
the barriers. In this way, I took the road back to Nyamata.

I returned to our family plot in Kanazi. The house had been
burned down. Neighbours explained that there was not a single
person left of my family. Through hearsay, I learned that Papa
had died near the house. Maman had been killed by a spear
thrown at her on the escape route to Burundi, I found two dead
sisters in the fields. As for the others, I received no information
as to how they had been killed.

I did not know how to do anything except farm, but the land
had become all too recalcitrant in my absence. I felt too weak
and too frail to plant beans. I was very demoralized. I heard
tongues wagging behind my back about my trip to the Congo, I
did not know which way to go looking for the slightest help:
this is why I moved to Nyamata, to an acquaintance's.

One day, I heard that the rains would carry off the bones of
people the bulldozers had buried by the church. I joined a team
to take the bones out of the hole and put them in safety. I was

looking for company, I wanted to look decent to others. Understanding locals brought sacks of cement and we made the Memorial. Now I try to work as a mason's mate here and there. When I earn a few coins, I buy potatoes and sorghum, and happiness comes back for a while. Otherwise, I go visiting a woman neighbour I am close to, or I wait for some passing luck. I feel disoriented to be the sole survivor in my family. I can no longer see in what direction to guide my life. I have a three year old boy – his name is Uwimana – and a three month old baby. They do not have Christian names because they do not have a father. Since the genocide, many girls have had children because there are many men roaming about who no longer have wives and they know of our desperate need for money.

The truth is that our minds are very muddled because we have lost our parents and our families. We have no one to obey, no one to look after, no one to confide in or ask for advice. No one scolds or encourages us anymore. We find ourselves without anyone with whom to imagine a destiny, without a shoulder to lean on of a sorrowful evening. It is such a great discomfort to live forsaken, it is a great distress to live in this way. Being solitary can even make you suspect. In Africa, even if you do not have a house, even if you no longer have a family, even if you cannot lift a hoe anymore, you must at least feed the children. Otherwise you very quickly lose your credit in other people's eyes.

At night, I think of my family with remorse. We had beautiful cows, we never wanted for clothes, we were several working the fields together, eating together, and we felt we were well supported. Today, there is too much emptiness and sorrow to be able to survive decently. In the evenings, I sit down with survivor neighbours and we talk to each other of the genocide. We fill in what happened, since each of us lived through it in different places. Me, I feel wary of talking about my bad life in the Congo, which is why I make little arrange-ments with the truth, as you know. This said, the more I hear fellows talk about the massacres in the commune, the more anxious I feel. The Hutus accuse the Tutsis of being too arrogant and too tall, but these are just words of envy concealed. In Kanazi, the Tutsis were neither prouder, nor richer, nor more learned than the Hutus, they had plots of the same size, it was only that they were more supportive to one another. It is traditional that we look after one another. The importance the Hutus attach to ethnicity is only a pretext for jealousy and greed.

When I pass through Kanazi, I see on their plots *interahamwe* who have returned from the Congo. I know that a small crowd of killers is due to come out of the prisons. There are many who will never confess, and they will want to be up to their tricks again, once they have got all their strength back. I heard too many boasts and vengeful words spoken in the camps. I know that the *interahamwe* hold sway over Hutu farmers' minds. They promise them our plots, they curse us to our faces.

Time passes, and hardly seems to change things. I do not know why God has let such a curse linger over the Tutsis' heads, but when I think about it, the ideas go clattering around in my head.

11

The lockers at the memorials

I n Nyamata and Ntarama, the only buildings fenced off
by railings bristling with spikes are the churches. It's
as if the two memorials built within their grounds need to be
protected better than any public building or villa.

The initiative to build the Nyamata Memorial was taken at
the first rainy season. The remains of people slaughtered around
the church, whom the killers had hastily buried with mechanical
diggers, had started to rise up out of the earth and were being
scattered in the run off. Wild dogs and cats had already started
to fight over the territory.

At the time, no one in the devastated town – neither local
notables nor the council – could finance the costly identification
of the victims. On their side, foreign donors were above all
concerned with the fate of the refugees in the camps. This is why
locals undertook, with the help of hoes, to exhume the remains
and store them out of the rain inside the church. As the months
went by, the number of corpses increased as more remains,
unidentifiable and dismembered, were discovered in the fields,
in ditches, in wells, in enclosures, in the woods and streams.
Thus the idea for a Memorial was born, "to try", according to
Innocent's expression "in spite of poverty, to restore some
dignity worthy of the name to the forgotten victims".

A plain sign planted in front of the railings announces the
Memorial. At the entrance to the church, the visitor is seized by
the acrid smell of death. The church's concrete nave is empty,

poorly lit by the rays of the sun which stream in through the holes in the roof. To the left, in the vaulted sacristy, on full display on a table, like some symbolic and macabre sculpture, lie the dried and mummified bodies of a mother and child entwined, in which have been left the wooden staves used to mutilate them to death.

The Memorial has been built behind the nave, in a sort of cellar. You go there down a concrete stairway; the light is pallid, the smell of death suffocating. On the last step you sit down and look at the remains stacked on the shelves. On the top shelf is a row of shrouded corpses of those brought back intact; skulls are placed on the shelf beneath; on a shelf lower down – sternums, then pelvises, femurs... You are of course fascinated by the many skulls. Their sockets seem to fix you with gazes come from the hereafter. Many of them bear fracture marks, sometimes knives are still embedded.

Sixty-four lockers, on four levels, contain the bones of a total of about twenty-five thousand victims. Beneath the church, a neon-lit crypt with tiled walls is nearing completion. In this less intense, more neutral atmosphere, some corpses are already on display for the benefit of emotional visitors.

Twenty kilometres further on, at the church of Ntarama, the militia didn't take the trouble to dig mass graves, because the church, built far away from their homes, wasn't on their usual route. Throughout the genocide, thousands of bodies were left in the open, abandoned. It was then too late for the survivors to come and collect the remains of parents or friends – because the rains and the animals had already got to work. Also, early on, the people protected the site with railings. Then, as a memory, they decided to leave it as it was. So they left all the bodies in the same positions as at the moment of death – like a Pompeian scene – heaped up between benches, at the altar, curled up along the walls, in their cloths, shorts, dresses, with their glasses, flip-flops, pumps, aprons, suitcases, basins, jugs, sheets, necklaces, foam mattresses, books, everywhere a strong smell of corpses.

Later, because of the prohibitive cost of embalming products, they constructed a shelter where a number of the skulls and bones strewn outside the church are stacked.

At the doors to the two abandoned churches, wardens take it in turns to receive countless personalities, Rwandan or foreign, and teams of journalists who now want to visit the sites. These wardens open for them voluminous visitors' books. You read a lot of sentences like: "Because we must never forget!"; "With you in these painful times!" and a stream of predictable: "Never again", already read elsewhere.

In Ntarama, one of the guides is called Marc Nsabimana. He is Hutu, a retired soldier. Shortly before the war, he had returned to farm a nearby plot. Married to a Tutsi woman, he tried to save her as well as several of his friends. Among Hutu villagers, he was the powerless witness to the killings in the church and the marshes. Since then, he has quit farming to dedicate himself entirely to the memory of the victims. Indifferent to the heat, he lives wrapped up in an anorak and nods his head, as he tirelessly repeats: "How was it possible, how was it possible?" You first think that this is a question addressed to the person he's talking to; then you realise it's addressed to himself. The other guide is called Thèrese. Herself a survivor from the church, she lives a little further away. She's more talkative and, outside her working hours, you can find her at Marie's *cabaret*, Widows' Corner, chatting with girlfriends over a Primus, especially about the day's visitors, their unease, their ceremonial costumes, the meanness or the generosity of their tips.

Sign of the times, or sheer coincidence, the *muzungu* have all but disappeared from the region, ever since the white priests were evacuated, thus triggering off the massacres in the churches. In Kinyarwanda, the word *muzungu* signifies the White man, especially out of the mouths of curious, amused and well-meaning kids as they hail one on his way. Linguistically, though, *muzungu* means "he who takes the place of". In Nyamata, with few exceptions, priests and experts and workers

117

from international organizations are Rwandan or African.

The faithful have reopened the doors of a long abandoned, rundown church in Nyamata. This is where Edith Uwanyiligira – and her lodgers Florence the cake-maker, Gaspard the captain of Bugesera Football club, Gorette the cook – now go to mass on Sunday morning and for vespers, to come together with all their friends in prayer and hymns.

Edith is a mother as cheerful as she is pious. Life's cares cannot dampen her good spirits and light-heartedness (in public at least). She devotes an enormous amount of time to her two children's education. Her living-room is always full of the faithful, the rooms she lets with erudite lodgers, her yard with chatty neighbours and churchgoers, her veranda with relatives, her garden with rowdy children from the neighbourhood. The day before the first massacres began, Edith left her home on a long flight through a devastated country – with her husband Jean de Dieu, with her boy Bertrand in her arms, and with a baby in her belly, who would later become the mischievous Sandra.

Edith Uwanyiligira
34 years, teacher and school bursar
Nyamata Gatare

First, Papa was deputy clerk in the administrative district of Kibwa, near Ruhengeri. He earned a good living, he was esteemed. Then in the night he was offloaded along with his family into the bush of Nyamata. Tutsis did not stop coming in from Byumba, Gikongoro, from everywhere – they helped frighten off the lions and elephants, they gathered under cardboard huts. This is how I came to be born on the hill of Ntarama.

As a little girl, I never knew what it was to be safe. When the *inkotanyi* from Burundi attacked Rwanda, the soldiers had to kill Tutsis, as punishment. Because the Bugesera shares a border with Burundi, they killed a more significant number here. Those killed were replaced by Hutu farmers soon afterwards. However, we lived cheek by jowl with them without trouble. I always had kind-hearted Hutu friends in our area.

The civil war embedded itself in the hills in the year 1991. In that year, my first baby did not manage to come through, and he died in my belly because the road to the hospital was too risky. This was the beginning of very perilous political years, during which men let rip with joy in their hearts.

When finally the president's plane crashed, three years later, the radio stations forbade us to go out. Right then, we did not know what to think of our fate, but the Hutus in our region – they too – were hesitating as to our fate; like us, they were waiting. Then we heard the burgomasters, the police, the local civil servants, going up and down the bush, encouraging the villagers with this variety of order: "What stops you from killing these Tutsis like they did in Kigali? They are cockroaches!", "There is no more room for Tutsis, you must kill them any way you can", "They are vipers, and now's the time to get rid of them. No one will be punished!" At the same moment, the *interahamwe* and soldiers from the barracks at Gako exerted themselves with the first lots of killing of those whose houses were daubed with paint. So after five days, our Hutu friends turned against their former Tutsi friends.

I was coming to the end of a pregnancy, I sought shelter at our Hutu neighbour's home, a friend of old. One morning, he said to me: "Edith, you are a sin which may become fatal. I do not wish to die on your behalf. Leave instantly for the bush." So on the 14th of April, I went with my husband down to the Akanyaru River; we gave the ferryman a handsome sum of money to cross the river and we set off on the road to Gitarama.

In Gitarama town centre, the killings were not yet under way, as people were not really aware of the extermination programme. The Hutus were still confused, their parties were quarrelling. They did not know who was supposed to start.

We were living outdoors one on top of the other near the market, eating a meagre sorghum dough; life was very hard. It was here I gave birth to my daughter Sandra, on the ground in the midst of people, without a roof to protect her from the sun, without even a tree to shelter me from men's gazes.

One day, the Hutus told us: "That's it, the killers are coming to get you." We took refuge in the Electrogaz factory. Young men arrived, they shouted at the factory police: "You are to deliver us up the Tutsis who are hiding behind your fence." The police raised their rifles. But when they had moved off, the brigadier was sweating too much, he showed us to a van and left us in a ditch. We set off again on the road to Kabgayi, my husband, my son, my newborn baby, two sisters, a little maid and me.

During our flight, we were speechless, like cowed people. Everywhere we went, we heard: "These are Tutsis. Why are they walking upright when they should be lying down dead?" or "Look at those Tutsis, how bad they smell. They must be killed, we have to get rid of them." Even the little pupils from primary classes who we ran into on the road threw stones at us, shouting: "There go Tutsis, there go cockroaches", and they ran off to warn their parents: "A group of Tutsis has just gone past, they come from the Bugesera, we know which way they are going..."

We felt no shame about our filth, about our misery, we only felt the humiliation of fear. We did not think of ourselves as dirty, as having no money, but we were afraid of losing our lives. So we trembled hearing such cries as these, since those who hurled them our way could kill us, in front of everyone, by the wayside even, as though it were nothing. Even though we felt guilty for not being able to give our children food, we feared dying first. Since a boy not even twelve years old could on a whim put a hole in you with a knife, without a scolding from his parents.

An overload of refugees was waiting for us in Kabgayi, and again we slept out under an open sky. Tutsi refugees fleeing the

genocide in their districts were mixed with Hutu refugees
fleeing the RPF as it advanced towards the border. So, one day,
it had to happen: Hutu refugees started killing Tutsi refugees to
interahamwe applause. In Kabgayi, there were Hutu ministers,
Tutsi civil servants, Hutu and Tutsi bishops and international
photographs come to take photographs, without any danger
to themselves, of how they were killing Tutsis in the streets.
It was a great misery to find even scraps to eat. We were
hungry, we were full of lice. But take note of this lesson from
Mother Nature; despite famine and all the microbes from the
infections, children refused to fall ill for fear of the threat of
killings!

In the first days of the month of June it was Satan's turn to
come to town. Here is what he ordered: every morning, soldiers
would park a bus near the camp and make Tutsis get aboard.
They started with important people – priests, nuns, teachers,
businessmen. They took fifty passengers away into the bush
and, in the evening, the bus came back empty. On the 29th of
June, they put my husband aboard. His name was Jean de Dieu
Nkurunziza, he was a brilliant intellectual and a very considerate man.

Ever since that day, every night when I find myself in bed, I
think of him. Next I think of my mother, of my father, of my
brothers and sisters, of my parents in law, of everyone who was
killed. Then I think once more of my husband who is dead,
until sleep is ready for me.

My husband and I always enjoyed the happiness of
newlyweds. We had loved each other since childhood. We grew
up five hundred metres apart, on the same hill. After secondary
school, our love was for real, we got married. The day of my
marriage, I was adorned in a white dress embroidered with lace
just as in the photos. There was a crowd of dashing and joyful
people. My husband and I loved one another to bits. I was
capricious, he loved me too much, he did not even want me to
do anything around the house. After secondary school, I

continued my studies in Kigali, then I went to live at my husband's house in Ntarama, where he was a teacher; and I taught in the primary school at Cyugaro. Truly, with my husband, and my parents and parents in law, who spoiled me a lot, I can say I was very well looked after.

The genocide made me, at the age of twenty-seven, both a widow and orphan. One thing that makes me sadder than sad is that I do not know how my husband died and that I did not bury him. This is what disturbs me night and day. Because they made him get on a bus, and no one can tell me how he was killed. If I had seen him dead, if I had some clues as to his final journey, his last words for his family, if I had put him in a Christian grave, then perhaps his disappearance could be borne more easily.

Four days after his death, RPF troops came into Kabgayi. I returned to Ntarama along a sad road. Because the neighbours had been killed, because my two older brothers had gone, because the house had been burned down, because the bush had got the better of the fields, I decided to settle in Nyamata. Today, I would not wish to live a single morning in Ntarama, for fear of meeting up with memories.

In Nyamata too, the dead were on display on the ground when I arrived; at the church, in the middle of the streets, in the undergrowth, in every dwelling. If you went into the fields looking for something to eat, you tripped over corpses; the same for the forest trails. The air you breathed was thick with death. People were not at all happy, they were plunged deep into the heart of a sad torment because they thought incessantly of those who had died before their very eyes. Many were suffering from stinking wounds; there was nothing left to eat, nothing left to trade, there were far too many problems and all too few solutions.

I too had to face a very arid life on my return. I had a child and a baby, orphans rushing about the yards from all sides, I was isolated, I fell ill, I could not get to the health centre because I had no transport, I could find nothing to help me get by. I wanted to let myself go, because life had become too bitter. So, I do not know how, I started to pray. I began shyly and I went into the church, I recited psalms, then I sang my lungs out. I understood that God was calling me because it was He who would sustain me from now on. That's it – I understood that I had been too selfish and naïve before, that God had wanted me to draw closer to him. I now know that thanks to Him I shall want for nothing and I no longer complain because my husband was killed. I did not think of God before, because I was coddled too much, but now He is going to help me and He is going to love me. This is my experience.

In the Bible, you read that the Jews of Egypt suffered greatly from the harshness and the labours forced on them by Pharaoh. There were many deaths too because of the mistreatment by the Egyptians. God heard their complaints, He listened to them, prepared them to return again to their good land of Canaan. As for the Tutsis of Rwanda, they had nothing so good along the way. I see no comparison between the Jews, who were God's people, and the Tutsis, who are chosen by no one. But because many of us were killed, because in spite of this we stayed alive when everyone wanted us to die, it helps us meet God.

There is another reason I would like to point out. During the genocide, the survivor lost his trust at the same time as he lost everything else, and this confuses him more than he realizes. He can doubt about everything – strangers, colleagues, even neighbouring survivors. Alone, he will struggle to regain enough of this trust in people again to return amongst others, but fortunately in this God can help.

According to me, there is nothing special about the Tutsis. With us, when Hutus came to visit our homes, there was not a single word which set us apart. Before, we were identical, except, of course, that herdsmen were Tutsis. A few Hutus bought cows too, but they called themselves Tutsi. It was during the last colonization that Whites spoiled Hutu hearts. According to what my grandparents told me, harmful lessons started in primary school. Whites told the Hutus: "Look at these Tutsis, they have a king, they have favourites, they have cows. They think they are superior, they are arrogant, they want you to become their servants." So the Hutus prepared their response. Ever since Independence, you have always had Hutu propagandists stoking up a spirit of mistrust and vengeance. The settlers never recommended genocide, because the very word itself was not taught then. But without a doubt Rwandan intellectuals worked on these bad lessons.

These days, when I listen to the radio, I hear that Whites shoot off in fighter planes the minute there is trouble in Iraq or in Yugoslavia. In Rwanda, people were bled for three months, and all the Whites sent were journalists on foot to take photos. Whites are as wary of the Tutsis as they are of the Jews. Their arms folded, they looked on as they died, almost to the last man – that's the truth. This is the real comparison between the genocides, and this problem will rise up again because their suspicions are lost at the bottom of their thoughts.

In Nyamata, it's a remarkable fact that people do not invite each other as before. Many people dried up inside for having suffered all too painful a trial during the war. They say: "The Hutus tried to kill me several times, now nothing more can happen to me." They think: "I am a widow, I am an orphan, there is no longer a place I can call my own, I no longer have a job, I no longer have transport, I have lost my health, I am alone up against too many problems and I do not want to see what goes on around me." Everyone has gone into their shells. Everyone goes into his corner, taking his own sadness, as if he were the sole survivor, no longer concerned that the pain is the same for everyone. Men are spending more hours than ever in the *cabarets*, but without any exchange of ideas. Women can wait in the house for a month without a family visit. A man can go three months without looking up a little sister for news and, if the news is not good, he can turn for home just like that. An attachment has been broken in families, as if people only want to use what remains of life for themselves.

For me, in my memory, the genocide is yesterday, or last year rather; and it will always be last year, because I can detect no change which will allow time to restore herself to her rightful place. Also, children are choosing the wrong path. Even school pupils who did not see the murders – they listen to conversation behind walls, they hear all sorts of curses, and afterwards you meet them answering grown-ups: "If you start giving me grief, I going to whack you with a machete" and in class they don't listen.

Understand well, the genocide is never going to recede from our minds. Time is going to keep these memories, it will give only a little room for the relief of souls. I found sanctuary in the church, since I could find nowhere else to hope. In church, I come across Hutus and Tutsis praying pell mell. I continue to rub shoulders with good Hutu friends. I know that all the Hutus who killed so calmly cannot be sincere when they ask for forgiveness, even from the Lord. For them, the Tutsi will always be their enemy.

But I am ready to forgive. It is not to deny the evil they did, it is neither a betrayal of the Tutsi nor the easy way out; it is so as not to suffer my whole life long asking myself why they wanted to cut me. I do not want to live off remorse and fear of being Tutsi. If I do not forgive them, I am the only one suffering, the only one who cannot sleep, who complains. I long for my body to be at peace. I truly must calm down. Even though I do not believe their soothing words, I must sweep fear far away from me.

I feel no need whatsoever to talk of the genocide all the time, like all the other survivors. When my boy Bertrand asks me: "Where's Papa?" I answer that he was killed. "By who?" "By the *interahamwe*." I explain that it was the *interahamwe* who killed his uncles and his grandparents in the marshes, in the fields, that these are very cruel men and women who shall never again wreak havoc. When he sees prisoners in uniform around a prison cell, he asks: "Are they the ones who killed Papa?" I answer him no, his papa was killed far from here by other *interahamwe*, that he must not look on these ones as criminals. To reassure him, I add: "We had to die because no one wanted us to live. We were meant to die because I was a woman with a child and a newborn baby who could not run. But we did not die, thanks to God." If he speaks to me of punishment, I answer that the genocide is beyond human laws. I answer that no justice is lucid enough to pronounce verdicts after such an event, only divine justice can do this. I try to satisfy him with this. I do not want the genocide to be read off my heart.

But I am also concerned for the new inhabitants, exiles who have come from Burundi to breathe life into the Bugesera; Hutus who did not dip their hands in the killings, little children born after the blood. We should not ruin their lives telling them our nightmares. I do not like to listen to all these memories about the killings which people keep repeating over and over in the evenings or in little groups at the weekend. I do not want to hear anything more about the marshes. I do not appreciate it when people come over to my house chatting about that time, always with more details of their misfortunes.

I do not want to be married again to a survivor, to resume a normal survivor life. I prefer prayer and songs. I prefer learning the guitar. I prefer to be in communion with heaven amongst friends. Every day I think of my husband in silence, I do not think there is a man who could ever offer me the happiness he gave me. I also think that if he had not been killed, I would not have met God.

I only agreed to talk to you about the genocide today because you have undertaken a long journey to come to Nyamata, because I have understood your need to hear about what we went through during this time, your desire to know how I am supposed to survive these sorrows.

12

A clarification along the way

At this stage of the book, the reader might well be surprised to be reading only stories of survivors. In Nyamata, as it happens, the burgomaster, the chief prosecutor, teachers returned from exile, former prisoners from Rilima, Hutu farmers – guilty or innocent, heroic or passive – and the survivors themselves all suggested I widen the range of statements. The reason why I refused is simple.

In Rwanda, at the beginning of the 1990s, in the wake of the first military breakthroughs on the part of the Uganda-based Tutsi rebellion, a majority faction of the political class, the army and the Hutu intelligentsia, worked out an extermination plan for the Tutsi population and for Hutu democratic personalities. From the 7th April, 1994, for four to ten weeks depending on the region, a surprisingly large part of the Hutu population grabbed hold, freely or by force, of machetes to kill. Foreigners, civil and military volunteers, humanitarian delegates, were sent to safety. Very rare, and very distraught were those journalists who ventured out onto the roads, and they were hardly believed on their return.

After May, the genocide gives way to a series of events which looked good on television: a Dantean exodus of around two million Hutus, overseen by *interahamwe* militia, who fled the reprisals. At the same time, the country falls to rebel RPF troops come from the Ugandan maquis. Then, thirty months later, in November 1996, the sudden and unexpected return of Hutu refugees, brought on by vengeful and very murderous raids, ostensibly for security purposes, on the part of RPF troops on the camps (and into the depths of the Kivu forest in the Congo).

Very few were the foreign journalists present in Rwanda during the Tutsi genocide (spring 1994), but a multitude landed in summer 1994 to follow columns of Hutu refugees to the Congo border. The lopsidedness of information – the flight of refugees, on unclear grounds, the drama of these long exhausting marches together with the harshness of the new leaders in Kigali gave rise to confusion in our western minds, to the point where the survivors of the genocide, still dazed in the bush, were practically forgotten and where Hutu refugees in their exodus on the roads and in the camps in the Congo were seen as the only victims.

During a trip to Rwanda in the middle of the exodus, I was struck by how withdrawn the survivors were in telling their stories. On a second trip three years later to Nyamata, their taciturnity bewilders me even more. The silence and isolation of the survivors in the hills is unsettling. As already noted in the introduction, I was reminded that only after a long period, when countless works by others on the Holocaust had already been published, were the survivors of the Nazi concentration camps themselves willing, and able, to be heard and read, and how crucial their stories were in trying to understand what had happened. During initial discussions with Sylvie Umubyeyi, and then with Jeanette Ayinkamiye and other people Sylvie had introduced me to, it immediately seemed obvious to me that I should spend time listening to them.

My stay in Nyamata lasts several months, broken up by trips to Paris to listen, at a distance, to the interviews and read notes, and then to come back out with new questions. There, a room in Edith's house, a four-by-four rented from Monsieur Chicago – one of the local beer merchants – and a tape recorder wait for me. Wake up call at dawn to the cries of a gang of kids, morning meeting with Innocent and Sylvie, excursions into the bush to visit one person or the other. Break at midday followed by an outing to the plots. End of the afternoon – free time to play with kids or transcribe word for word the interviews recorded, out of interest for the contents and for the pleasure of the music of the voices. In the evening, beers at a *cabaret*, Sylvie's, Marie Louise's, Francine's in Kibungo and Marie's at Kanzenze, to chat with friends. The weekend is given over to writing, to listening to a church choir and to watching a football match. Unexpected encounters, Raymond Depardon's friendly visit, or festivities sometimes interrupt this spartan schedule.

Basically, I came looking for survivors' stories, on the hills and in the valleys of the marshes and banana groves. These narratives are essential to our understanding of the genocide. Their truth is unaffected by the fact that, as the survivors point out themselves, memories can be inaccurate, contain mistakes. This is why interviews with political or legal personalities, from Kigali or Nyamata, or the stories of killers and former *interahamwe* chiefs (recorded in the prison at Rilima or abroad) are not included here.* For the same reason, excluded also are interviews with Hutu resistants and foreign protagonists.

After this clarification, we now return to a track through a eucalyptus forest close to Ntarama, where trills the *inyombya*, a bird with a long blue tail. We climb up a steep path which disappears into a half wild banana grove. Exuberant kids spring out from behind a hedge. In the yard, a young woman wearing a field cloth is having a rest, leaning against the wall of the house, legs stretched out, a baby asleep on her lap. Her name is Berthe Mwanankabandi.

She offers water from a large jug. Like others, she's surprised that a foreigner should be interested in her story and in the genocide; she explains, like others, that she no longer believes in the benefits of bearing witness, but there's nothing suspicious –

*These are the subject of my book, *A Time for Machetes*.

on the contrary – in her way of expressing herself. In a quiet voice, she immediately agrees to talk, for the entire morning.

Like many of her neighbours, she never complains, never raises her voice, shows neither hatred nor bitterness, disguises any wariness towards a White and in silence contains onsets of sadness or distress. In the afternoon, when it's time to go back to the fields to work, she offers to continue her story another time. The following week, then one, two, six months later, she is just as focused, because, as she explains herself, speaking out loud clarifies some of her thoughts.

Berthe Mwanankabandi
20 years old, farmer
Hill of Rugarama (Kanzenze)

I was born in the midst of two brothers and nine sisters. When we were small, we walked through the forest in a children's procession to the school in Cyugaro. On the benches, there was no place for ethnic responses. Even when there were disturbing massacres in the area around Rulindo, it was forbidden to swap testimonies amongst ourselves. Even if you could hear young men in battle training near the Akanyaru bridge, it was forbidden to express surprise. We wrapped our fears in leaves of silence.

The day the plane crashed, we huddled up in our houses; we could hear groups of *interahamwe* hunting from hill to hill, in an uproar. In the banana grove below the house, I heard news that they had killed our old neighbour, whose name was Candali. We immediately went down in a family procession to the church in Ntarama; supposedly Christians respected places of worship. We waited three days for spirits to calm down. We actually believed that we would soon be returning to our land, but this time the *interahamwe* came.

In the little church wood, they gathered a circle of young

men; then they began to smash holes in the walls with grenades and they entered singing songs. At first we said to ourselves that they had gone mad. They were brandishing machetes or axes and spears and yelled: "Here we are, here we are, and this is how we prepare Tutsi meat."

Behind the church, the boldest amongst us slipped through the trees in the park. We ran without thinking and finally reached the marshes of Nyamwiza. That evening, the rain poured down incessantly, and we sought refuge in the school at Cyugaro, in the eucalyptus wood not far from the marshes. This was our route for a month; the marshes, school, the marshes. It was in this school that I later found out how Papa and Maman had sighed their last breath. To the very end they pined for their native hill near Byumba, where their home was stolen from them before they came here to grow beans on a plot.

Every morning I would prepare the children a meal with food dug from the ground; then I took them out early to hide under the papyrus leaves in the company of adults who had used up all their energy. On sunny days, I had to change places because of the footprints left behind in the dry mud. When the massacrers arrived, they were singing; then it was our turn to scatter into the marshes. They came at around nine o'clock or sometimes at ten or eleven, if they did not want to work too much. Some days they were disguised as devils, with cloths on their shoulders, with leaves in their hair. Sometimes they tried to surprise us by arriving in silence, but the cries of the fleeing monkeys gave them away.

When they caught a family, they struck the papa first, the maman second, then the children, so that everything was as it should be. They left promptly at half past four because they wanted to be home before nightfall.

It was then that the lucky runaways came out and started scouring the hiding places, trying to find those who had been killed. The most courageous went up to the school for shelter and to enjoy a little communal life. The weakest simply lay

down to dry out beneath the nearest trees. As for us, because our house was nearby, we roamed about the plots at night, laying in food. We tried to give news about neighbours we had seen during the day.

In the marshes the acquaintance you had been hiding with day in, day out, might vanish one evening, and you did not know whether she had escaped with another group or whether she had been cut down. You knew nothing about many of those who were absent. You would run into them again the next day, or they had already come to a sticky end.

I have to say that little by little we got used to not knowing anything about our acquaintances because we had more pressing concerns, about how, right now, not to get caught with one group. We sometimes did not notice that someone we had sat with on the school benches or with whom we had shared the *urwagwa* for years had vanished. For a small number of people even, dejection destroyed feelings of friendship and familiarity. With all the misery and fear, it became difficult for them not to think about themselves the whole time.

After the cooking chores were done, we huddled up together or looked after the injured. Lack of food and sleep meant that times were hard in the marshes; we were laid low by dysentery and all sorts of stagnant water diarrhoea. Malaria, on the other hand, usually so tenacious, proved on the contrary to be merciful, and this still surprises me. And not only malaria, since very few of the friends around me were complaining of the customary ailments – of the head, the belly or, for women, the groin. In the midst of all our misfortunes, these illnesses seemed to be offering us out of solidarity a little period of grace.

The evening of the 30th of April, I discovered the bloody remains of Rosaline and Catherine, my two little sisters. That night, I was wild with grief. After this in the marshes, wisdom sometimes took leave of me when I saw they had killed little children or close neighbours, or when I heard the groans of those who had been chopped.

I caught myself wishing to die. But I never got up out of my hiding place when I spied the hunters. When they came, I could not command my muscles, they refused to move. At the very last minute, they would not agree to my making a move so that a killer could come and slice my head off. Like other people you saw through the branches who could not stop themselves from raising a hand one last time over the head, fending off the machete blow which would have killed them straight off; even though, in doing so, the multiple wounds would make their suffering much longer lasting. In our deepest core is the will to survive that listens to no one.

When the *inkotanyi* freed us one afternoon, they escorted us – a flock of filth – to Nyamata. I can find no other words. I was dressed like a thief, in rags and scraps of fabric scratched by branches. We walked in a slow-motion dream because although we were walking in broad daylight, we did not run for fear of being chopped down.

In the evening, in Nyamata, some young men caught a goat, lit a fire and handed me a kebab. So I tasted grilled meat again – I took my time, ate very slowly; I calmly lay down on a mattress, closed my eyelids, then I felt that once again I was myself.

I lasted three months in the camp. I was nearly empty of ideas, I could no longer feel my intelligence working. Above all, I dozed. The liberators told us that the threat of massacres had gone away from our lives forever, that we had won. But amongst ourselves we said quietly that we did not know what we were supposed to have won because we had lost what was most important. Then I decided to take the road to Rugarama and return to the house, even though my parents would never come back. I ventured out into the hills with neighbours, looking for sheet metal and doors that the fleeing Hutu had abandoned beneath the trees. The bush was eating up the cultivations from all sides, the plots had to be put to work again, it was all very dispiriting, but there were children pushing us on.

Counting those at Claudine's next door, eight little children took the path back to school in Ntarama, and four big ones went to work in the fields, except those who had a baby to look after. As for me, I got a baby from a man passing through. The child is called Tuyishime, which means Son.

Every morning, we grown-ups leave for the fields at six and come back at around eleven to heat up some food. We wash and get ready for a little nap, we go back out and fulfil our chores and come back around five o'clock to get water. If the genocide had not stopped me, I would have been a nurse. I feel a great yearning for this position and its benefits.

With us, memories of the genocide come up in conversation at any moment. But over time, I am less and less able to summon up images from the marshes, faces of the unlucky ones, the mud, the twists of fate of this life of genocide. More and more I see life as it formerly was, in the family, in the company of the living, around the house and on the hill tracks. It comes back to me how beneficial life was amongst my parents and neighbours. But to remember the good times of before does not ease my sorrow. On the contrary I think that the person who remembers nothing but the genocide, who thinks only of this, who speaks only of this, is bathed in sorrow but at least is less overcome with regrets and worries.

I see that life in the hills now is too back breaking, the earth has become too hardened for hope to flower. The genocide drives towards isolation those it did not drive towards death. There are some who have lost the taste for kindness. She who gave birth to her children and saw them killed, he who built his house and saw it burnt, he who put his beautifully coloured cattle out to pasture and who knows they were boiled up in a pot – how can you imagine them getting up in the mornings, with nothing in their hands? There are even some who have become quite crazed. For example, if your cow goes eating in someone else's field, he will scream at you that he will refuse to come to any settlement over damages because he has lost all his own, and he will threaten you for nothing at all.

It is the young children who grieve me the most though. They saw all these dead around them, they are afraid of everything and anything and as for the rest they don't care. One day I even heard children playing at being *interahamwe* and threatening to kill each other. These are dreadful shadows which come back to their minds in disguise.

Formerly, with neighbouring Hutu folk, we never used to offer gifts, but we shared the local drink together and spoke properly to each other; and there you go, one day all of a sudden they called us "snakes". It became a serious accusation, which perhaps got the better of them.

During the massacre in the church at Ntarama, I recognised two Hutu neighbours killing like champions – they died in the Congo. In the marshes I also recognised a farmer from the neighbourhood; during the killings he worked with a spear. He was in the flight to the Congo, he came back two years later; he waited for the soldiers at his house and told them that he remembered nothing of what he had done. He was condemned to death. I do not know if they are going to shoot him on the hill one day, in any case I shall not go out of my way to find out. Because nothing of all this brings me relief.

This is what I think. Those who only wanted to steal our land could have simply chased us out, as they did to our parents and our grandparents in the North. Why cut us as well? There are Hutus who cut the throat of their Tutsi wives and children, who were only half Tutsi. Many did not try to hide their misdeeds. On the contrary, some even killed at the doors of houses in front of a small audience, to prove that they were trustworthy Hutus and have the *interahamwe* pay them compliments.

Before, I knew that one man could kill another, because there were killings all the time. Now I know that even the person with whom you have shared food, or with whom you have slept, can kill you without embarrassment. A bad person can kill you with his teeth, that is what I have learned since, and I no longer set my eyes on the face of the world in the same way.

When I hear news about all these African wars on the radio, I fear that the end is near for Africa. African leaders make decisions on affairs all too brutally. It is an insurmountable problem for us, the little people. But the case of Rwanda escapes African customs. An African massacres with anger or hunger gnawing his belly. Or he massacres as much as is necessary to confiscate diamonds or suchlike. He does not massacre on a full stomach and with his heart at peace on hills planted with beans like the *interahamwe*. I think they mislearned a lesson from somewhere else, from out of Africa. I do not know who sowed the idea of genocide. No, I do not say it was the settler. Really, I do not know who it was, but it is not an African.

I do not understand why the Whites watched us for such a long time, while every day we suffered the blades. If you who witnessed the genocide on your television screen do not know why the Whites did not raise a hand in protest, how was I, buried in the marshes, supposed to know?

I do not understand why certain suffering faces, like those of Hutus in the Congo or the fugitives in Kosovo, touch foreigners and why Tutsi faces, even carved by machetes, provoke only thoughtlessness and neglect. I am not sure I understand or believe in a foreigner's pity. Perhaps the Tutsis were hidden too far from the road, or perhaps their faces did not adequately express this type of feeling.

In any case, what the Hutus did is without question devilry. This is why, as long as there are *interahamwe* and their supporters incarcerated in Tilima, I will still tremble when I hear voices speaking from amongst the leaves in the banana groves.

13

Claudine's mud and tin house

The track that leads to Claudine Kayitesi's home climbs a steep, clay slope, disappears into the tangles of a banana grove and comes out onto a flower hedge. Her small house is a non-durable construction. In the Bugesera, the various ways of building walls classifies houses as non-durable, semi-durable and durable, which is to say: dried mud bricks slapped onto a frame fashioned out of tree trunks; sun-dried bricks made of mud mixed with straw and coated with cement; and baked bricks or cement blocks. Roofing is most often odd-sized strips of sheet metal, held down with stones, or else new, screwed down and jointed. Claudine's house, the work of her father a dozen years ago, has deep cracks all over. However, unlike Berthe's, her friend and neighbour's house, hers doesn't flood during the wet season.

You enter a white-washed room, furnished with a coffee table and two chairs, decorated with several seasonal flower bouquets. This is where the family waits out the rain showers. A strip of fabric separates the living area from the back room, furnished with two plank beds. On a table there's a bible, a basket of artificial communion flowers, a charcoal iron, and a sewing kit. This is where Claudine and her little sister Eugenie, who helps her bring up the children, sleep. On the right, a windowless store cupboard houses sacks of beans, sachets of salt, rice, a jug, a bar of soap. No trace of a bag of sweets or biscuits. A travel bag filled with clothes stands in for a wardrobe. The store cupboard gives onto a third room. A mattress covers a bed base moulded out of the earth floor. Here sleep the children, Jean-Petit, Joséphine and tiny Nadine, only a few months old.

Unlike at Berthe's or Jeanette's, no image, calendar or old advertisement poster decorate the walls. The earthen floor and the yard are kept meticulously clean with the help of a broom made from leaves.

Outside, a superb, rustic style, chaise longue and a bench runs along the wall. It's here where you chat when it's not raining. The yard is round and huge. It's protected by a euphorbia hedge on which some fabrics and washing dry. In the shade of avocado trees, a square lawn surrounded by flowerbeds and overhung with perfumed, yellow shrubs hosts evening gatherings. Further on, an openwork fence made from branches is used as a shelf for an array of pots, cups, Thermos flasks, and gifts from humanitarian organizations, as well as buckets which, at bath time, are filled and used to douse each other with. The kitchen can be found in a mud shack with a tin roof, where there is only room enough to sit down. On a wood fire bananas and beans cook in an enormous metal pot, to be served up for the two daily meals. Tomorrow it's manioc and beans, corn and beans the day after. For the Rwandans, a day without beans is a day gone wrong.

Beside the kitchen, the enclosure for the cow and calf is made from thick branches planted into the earth. The cow is thin because when the children come back from school, they don't have the time to take her out and let her graze her fill. She produces little milk. With less than four, five cows, it's not profitable to hire a young cowherd. Claudine explains that she can't risk having her cow slip in with another cattleman's herd, because in the case of mischief in the field, she wouldn't be able to pay the damages. The calf is no plumper than its mother, but is lively. On the dung hill, two or three hens peck at each other, their chicks barely surviving the wild cats. Behind the kitchen, at the edge of the banana grove, a clay hut with a metal roof is the outhouse.

The houses nearest are Berthe's and, three hundred metres further down the track, Gilbert and Rodrigue's, two adolescent brothers who survived side by side in the marshes. Six hundred metres from Claudine's is the spring.

At twilight, the family meets round a petrol lamp cobbled together from a metal gourd and an oakum wick. From morning to evening, the house is cheered up by an amazing concert of playful and languorous birdsong. Despite which, Claudine dreams of having a radio cassette player, or at least a radio, to make the long shadowy evenings more pleasant. She also dreams of having a bicycle so she can transport her water canisters, bring back the shopping from Ntarama, take bunches of bananas down to market and above all go to Nyamata more often, to visit people and to have some good times.

Neither the drought which sears her banana grove, nor the cares of her large family, nor the harshness of "men's" work, can draw out of her the least complaint or undermine her touching sense of humour.

Claudine Kayitesi
21 years old, farmer
Hill of Rugarama (Kanzenze)

It is a fact that that the genocide in our country began on the 11th of April at eleven in the morning and ended on the 14th of May at two in the afternoon. I was in my eighth and final year at school in Nyirarukobwa when it hit us. It taught me two lessons. The first is that there is no word in Kinyarwandan to describe the crimes of the killers of a genocide, a word whose meaning can outdo the wickedness, the ferocity and the category of actual feelings. I do not know if you have a word for this at your disposal in the French language.

The second lesson is a bitter one for me, although it is not that serious. It is that since the genocide some of survivors, sometimes those who suffered greatly, can quarrel, yes they too, over silly things like envy. Even though together they shared raw manioc and a terrible fate, even though they scratched the lice and the vermin out of one another's hair and off each other's backs, close knit like children from a big family, misery and ingratitude can drive them apart. As if the all too necessary fraternity of the marshes dried up all possibility for kindness and mutual help.

Before the fatal month of April, our farmers were concerned about the evil ear of war. When we went to draw water, we heard Hutu neighbours spicing up their conversations in this way: "The Tutsis have started to crawl like snakes, they will end up beneath our feet" and other such intimidations. Joyful troops were chanting threats on the road. In their hands I saw shining machetes which had never got dirty in a banana grove, so I expected the situation would rapidly deteriorate.

When news came of the plane crash, I joined some fugitives in the forest of Kinkwi. We tried to defend ourselves by throwing stones. But our courage deserted us and we left the land and took refuge with everyone else in the church. When the first grenade exploded, I was most fortunately near the back door, and I managed to slip away. I knew that the hills were overrun by *interahamwe*, so without turning back I ran for the marshes. I could hear other fugitives in the thicket. We knew about the marshes by reputation. We had never gone there before because of the mosquitoes, snakes and the mistrust they cast as far as the eye can see. That day, without slowing our pace a single step, we belly-flopped into the mud.

That night, the eucalyptus forest seemed quiet, so we walked to Cyugaro. Little by little, the luckiest fugitives from the banana groves joined us. Our survival routine repeated itself. At dawn, we went down into the marshes and squeezed our way through the papyrus. So as to avoid dying all together, we split up into small teams. We put three children here, two

children further on, two more in another place. We multiplied
our chances, we curled up in a sleeping position in the mud,
wrapping ourselves in leaves. Before the attackers arrived, we
swapped ideas to give fear the slip; afterwards we would not
even be able to whisper. We drank marsh water full of mud.
It was fortified, pardon the expression, by the blood of corpses.

We had no trouble hearing the *interahamwe* from far off.
They sang and whistled, they fired gunshots into the air, but
they were careful not to waste any bullets when they killed
people on the spot. During the first days, they crouched down
and whispered friendly words, in order to bait us: " "Little one,
come out, come out, Maman, we can see you…" Well, even
those who were so frightened they could do nothing but obey
were not even rewarded with a quick bullet. Which is the
reason why later neither the sick, nor the infants, nor anyone
stirred until the whistle to leave rang out.

In the evening, as Berthe has outlined, we prepared food for
the children, we ate as much as we could find: manioc, sweet
potatoes, bananas, to fortify ourselves and to survive into the
next day. Since we could not take anything with us during the
day, we lined our bellies, if I may put it thus. We put the
children to sleep in the pen, or in the kitchen, never in the
house. We spoke in quiet voices so as not to arouse the killers'
curiosity. We described the corpses we had seen during the day,
how they had been chopped; we counted those not present at
the edge of the marsh, and so deduced who had been caught
during the day. We wondered who would be killed the next day.
After the first killing sessions, we no longer asked ourselves
why we had to die. This question had become insignificant. But
we thought a lot about the how of it. We tried to imagine
suffering death under the machete. In any case, it was
something that I was greatly concerned about.

We never found any cause to squabble, since all we thought
of was death and the need to help one another. We slept in
turns. Around five o'clock in the morning, we would start down

the road, very quietly because we knew the *interahamwe* were dozing. We waited for sunrise at the edge of the marsh and for the attacks which would begin again. We wore the same torn garments. We did not suffer from a sense of indecency because we knew we were all alike. We helped one another to pluck the tons of lice from our hair. The mosquitoes did not think twice about stinging us occasionally, but, in a certain way, our muddy filth was a protection against malaria. Thus we endured this wild existence. Time had forgotten us. It was passing for other people, for Hutus, foreigners, animals, but it no longer wished to pass for us. Time neglected us because it no longer believed in us, and we, as a result, hoped for nothing from time. So we expected nothing.

On certain days, when they had caught a little group, they would take a girl away with them, not killing her immediately, and force their will upon her at home. This is how, thanks to their beauty, some girls stayed alive for a few extra nights. It is a custom with men in our country not to kill the girl they have themselves penetrated, because they fear it is a curse to mix these two sorts of feelings. After this, though, another of their fellows would chop the girls and dump their bodies into the ditches.

Some days, the Hutus would work mainly on the other side of the marsh, so we were able to chat and eat a little scrap of survival. The next day, they would work very hard on our side; so we did not even dare breathe and the children risked being devoured by hunger.

The criminals did not bury their victims, because the great numbers put them off. They preferred to get the job of killing done, without the additional fatigue of wiping away the traces. These people were so sure they would get rid of all Tutsis that they concluded that no one would ever come and interfere with their business in Rwanda.

On the 30th of April precisely, they came down from every road. They attacked from all sides, they formed a very excited mob; they had a vast programme of killing which would go on all day without a midday break. That evening, there were thousands of corpses and dying people, in the bottom of the ponds, all over the place; I was so dejected I thought about forgetting myself lying in the marsh water, but I still did not dare wait for the machete. I know no one who took his own life. I think we were too concerned with surviving to waste time over such thoughts. I have never met anyone who says he is ashamed to be a survivor; only a few people who feel ill at ease, for example, on a day they fail to do an essential task they could have done.

To hear Whites talking, the genocide is supposedly a madness, but this is not that true. It is a job meticulously prepared and efficiently carried out. To hear Hutu neighbours, they supposedly killed a few people themselves under threat of death; this is true for a small number only. When a farmer is lazy, his field is never green; when a driver is negligent, his truck breaks down; but in the marshes, you could count dozens of corpses without noticing any laziness or negligence on the part of our Hutu compatriots.

The truth is that a great number of Hutus could no longer bear the Tutsis. Why? This is a long-running question which haunts every banana grove. As for me, I see there are differ-.ences between the Tutsis and Hutus, which make the latter all too mistrustful. Tutsis are sometimes shaped with more slender necks and straighter noses. Thus, they have thinner faces. They are more sober in character and more reserved. A Hutu would never be afraid of turning up at the door of an office or a health centre wearing his field clothes; but a Tutsi would change his clothes. As for wealth and intelligence though, there is no difference. Many Hutus are wary of a supposed malice in the Tutsi character or spirit, but this just does not exist.

The Hutus also say we owned too many cows – this was not true. My parents did not raise any cattle. Our neighbours did not have cows, and they were more numerous and needier. At the market cows wait on whoever can buy them with money. The truth is that Hutus do not like the company of cows. When a Tutsi comes across a herd of cows in a grove, he sees good fortune. When a Hutu comes across cows, all he sees are hooves and hassle.

The Hutus also mutter that Tutsis are arrogant, that they do not want to marry Hutus, do not want to offer Hutu families a dowry. But if Hutus start killing Tutsis in the neighbourhood, a Tutsi girl who has followed her husband to a Hutu hill is not going to feel safe and so, alone and with nothing, she will return to her family.

As for me, I think that Hutu extremists cut down the Tutsis simply because they wanted to trim the women to size; being too tall for their liking, they wanted to eat their herds which ate too much grass, and grab their land. Which is why without reason they accuse them of being swarming cockroaches.

I often think that we are the forgotten of Africa. We live in the Africa of the French, but the French view kindly only the Hutus. I do not know why Whites are mistrustful of Tutsis. Perhaps because the Tutsis have developed their own education for themselves and they are less natural. I see that Whites are scandalized by the genocide, but with their backs turned they say that the Tutsis brought it upon themselves with their behaviour towards the Hutus and other such beliefs. Whites do not want to see what they cannot believe, and they cannot believe in a genocide because it is a killing that is beyond everyone's understanding, including them.

But we must nevertheless remember a much more important truth, our African brothers did nothing more than the Whites to save our lives, and yet no one better than a Black can understand the misfortunes of another Black, because of common customs and inherited languages. Because of this dryness in the heart, we will always remain alone up in the hills in the midst of murky threats.

But nevertheless, I congratulate myself on being Tutsi, because otherwise I would be Hutu.

Only once did I return to the marshes with a girlfriend to see these mud hiding places where we lived, the ponds where all these neighbours expired. Then I simply never went back. Often, at night, images crowd in as dreams; I see faces again that look at me without saying a word, and when I wake up, I feel disquiet between me and those who were cut. No, I do not feel I am to blame. I am not at fault, because there was nothing I could for them. Nevertheless I am not made happy by the luck I had. I do not know how to explain this feeling, because it touches on very intimate relationships between myself and people who are no longer alive. I am embarrassed and very anxious when I think of them. I am not just sad as after an ordinary death.

I work in agriculture so as to give the children food. There are ten of us without parents in the two houses, and I am the eldest. A woman neighbour found one of our cows, she has since borne us a calf, she provides some milk for the little ones and manure for the banana grove. On Saturdays, I assist a mason in Ntarama to earn a few pennies, I get assistance from the Survivor's Fund.

When I walk past the Memorial church, I do not like to look at all these nameless bones. But I do sometimes accompany foreign visitors who have erred on the road, and then I cannot help but stare at the skulls. I am made uncomfortable by the feeling these hollowed-out eye sockets convey, of people who are perhaps not at rest, after what they suffered, and who cannot bury their humiliation beneath the earth.

Often, when the *interahamwe* had killed a person, they would take their clothes if in good condition. When we encountered these totally naked corpses which had been chopped in pieces, those of old people, those of young girls – those of everyone, this vision of nakedness brutally seared the nerves. These naked bodies abandoned to time were no longer themselves, nor were they already us. They were truly a nightmare I do not think you could understand.

Sometimes, I go to a church to pray, because I had the opportunity to be baptized. I ask of God only one thing now: to help me not become wicked towards those who did all this evil to us. Nothing more, really. I do not want to taste revenge.

I cannot for definite say that I shall never marry. But what man would want to give his money to feed all these orphaned children who eat in my house? In Africa, when you live in misfortune, a friend will bring you a drink; he will comfort you with soothing words, he will take all the time it needs to raise your spirits, he will take care of your health if you are suffering from fever; but the gift of money is very different. In Africa, family blood is very important when it comes to sharing material things. Outside the family, we are more inclined to exchange a few kind words than a few bank notes.

I often see myself as I was before, with Papa and Maman, with brothers and sisters, I think of the school benches, of books I stroked with the flat of my hand, of the career as a teacher I envisaged for myself, and I struggle to sustain a taste for life. Before, I used to love reading stories in books. Today, time hardly comes to my aid, I can no longer find the opportunity, and I do not come across a single copy of a book. I do not think the genocide changed my personality, except that I greatly suffer loneliness, and this can trouble me. When I find myself too isolated, in the midst of sad thoughts, I get up and go to see my neighbours, orphaned children like ourselves, and we listen to plays on the radio. I like them very much. They make us imagine faraway characters and all their dalliances.

Despite everything, I think it is beneficial to talk of what happened. Even if for us survivors it is painful to stir up such memories in front of strangers, and even if the truth cannot penetrate hard hearts. But I cannot help you with any very useful explanations as to the origins of the genocide.

I also think that no one will ever write all the ordered facts about this mysterious tragedy; neither professors from Kigali or Europe, nor intellectuals or politicians. Any explanation as to what happened will fall down one side or the other like a rickety table. A genocide is not a bad patch of scrub rising from two or three roots, but it is a cluster of roots which have gone rotten underground without anyone noticing.

I do not waste any more thoughts trying to understand my former neighbours. I sometimes joke about it all, to show willing, while my lips know that they are lying to my heart. I am very shaken by this curse, but I bottle it up within, I stop it from spilling out – I remain calm for the children.

14

Twilight at La Permanence

In Nyarunazi in the evening, a little after the sun has plunged into the marshes of Rulindo beyond the Akanyaru river, men come out of their homes and meet up in the former grain storehouse. They sit on the ground on low stools or lean against the wall. One of them sets a jerry can of *urwagwa* down in the middle of the room and sticks a reed into the spout. In turns, the men crouch down by the jerry can and suck in large gulps. In the darkness they chat about the pre-war period when Nyarunazi, near a rubber forest half way between Ntarama and Kibungo, was a boomtown. They also talk of women who are no longer there, of those who are not the same as before. They tease the mechanic who has just sold off his last jack and joke about the radio which has just packed in with flat batteries. Then they drink without talking anymore and later doze against the warehouse wall or go staggering home.

The stars in the limpid sky are the hamlet's only lights. On the path which goes down from Nyarunazi to the large track, silent silhouettes pass in small groups. Sometimes they talk in very quiet voices, as though they feared disturbing the sleep of the banana groves. In Bugesera in the middle of the night, even the narrowest path is not deserted. People are always going back up to their hills. Civil servants held up by a meeting, jackets slung over shoulders, farmers held back in the cabaret for a last Primus, women slowed down by children slumped on their backs or by sacks of beans piled up on their heads. Amidst the strident *tio ooo* of night gonoleks and the bellowing of cattle, the cuckoo's insistent call comes through. Many old villagers, leaning on a stick, the woman behind the man, have been walking slowly since the beginning of the afternoon. Others are already leaving in the night to catch at dawn a truck for Kigali.

On the approach to Nyamata, in the Gatare district, a sonorous cacophony of frogs croak back and forth from marsh to marsh. Red embers illuminate gatherings in yards, children wander through the bushes. On the football fields kids are playing in the darkness around a single goal, enjoying as long as possible a real football made from leather strips, lent them by their elders until the following morning.

In the main street, red dust falls along with the night as the wind drops. The remaining vehicles are parked behind fences. Tied to a string, the goats from the small market sleep. On the square, youths chat or listen to music in front of hairdressing salons. Mopeds transport couples clinging to each other out of love or because of jolts on the potholed road. Pale neon strips light the *cabarets*. Sitting beneath an awning, Monsieur Chicago supervises the stacking of beer crates in his warehouse. Monsieur Chicago is one of the few stout men in town, which is doubtlessly where he gets his nickname and cheerfulness from. With an opener he uncaps bottles and slips them into your hand as if stolen. He survived the massacres by walking all the way across the country from Gikongoro, a city in the south where he had a business which he never returned to.

Opposite the crossroads Théoneste's new van, the first since the war, is parked. Théoneste wears a moustache and "Kigali diaspora" style clothes. He was once the region's most popular tailor, when leading citizens wore his chic suits, their wives his bubus. He was part of the Kayumba forest group along with Innocent, Dominique, one of the directors at the re-education centre, and Benoît, the debonair cowboy... these twenty odd runners who survived. Théoneste pulled off the almost unique feat of escaping the hill and reaching the border with Burundi on his third attempt. From this miraculous exploit he no doubt derives his wild infectious laughter. His bazaar is never bereft of drinkers. An arcade further on, neon letters announce the entrance to Club, a meeting point for young people from well-to-do Burundi families, who melancholically relive the Bujumbura nights.

Still in the main street, a blue sheet stretched between two poles announces the opening of a new restaurant, La Permanence. The walls are painted in jade green, the tables are covered in embroidered cloths. The owner is Sylvie Umubyeyi. She comes in the evening only, has a bit of a chat with guests and keeps an eye on the business, because in the daytime she disappears into the bush.

As of the first meeting, Sylvie's black eyes reveal a strange serene and glittering beauty. The delight of her voice intensifies her charm, as does her elegant turn of phrase, as when, for example, you ask her for the secret of such pretty sentences and she answers: "It just flows, because if you have returned from down there, you have journeyed into the quick of life."

Sylvie is a survivor from Butare, a university town in the south west of the country. On arriving in Nyamata, at the end of the genocide, she knew no one in the town, even less so in the devastated surrounding areas, deserted or peopled by the dead. Since then, she has been a social worker in these hills, where, with her team every morning, she does a unique job.

She leaves early in a van through the fields and the undergrowth, goes through the banana groves, strikes out into the forest, looking for children who came out of the marshes alive, or came back from the camps in the Congo, hidden behind walls of clay and straw, wandering through the bush or the bean fields. She visits them, registers them, starts a dialogue and moves on.

When she comes up to a mud hovel, she politely calls out and announces herself, shakes hands with all the children who come running in from the surrounding plots and groves. She visits pens, inspects a leak in a sheet metal roof, checks uniforms and school copy books, asks about the hens, talks with the children and youth about seed, insomnia, running away. She sits on a tree trunk, chatting in a calm, cheerful voice, listens without bothering about the time. A leather-bound notebook and a Bic pen which she fiddles with are her work tools. Beneath her joyful exterior, Sylvie proves to be pragmatic, demanding and meticulous.

With her savings, she has bought a cow for each of her five children and has recently opened La Permanence to support her extended family which lives in her house. She is overflowing with energy because she loves her work. She is always well-turned out because she doesn't "stop caring with age", and wears a different outfit – a floral dress, tight jeans or a multicoloured cloth – every day. She is light-hearted and amazingly insightful about the world around her. As she tells her story, she sometimes pinches the bridge of her nose and closes her eyes, listens for a long moment to the crickets, so as to hold back tears.

Sylvie Umubyeyi
34 years old, social worker
Nyamata Gatare

For the journey we assembled as three or four families in a large vehicle and we followed the road for Kirundo. June was coming to an end. I was a survivor from Butare, but I did not carry along with me the hope that I could go on all the way home, because the killings had not ended there.

In those days, it was still unthinkable to travel to whichever district you wanted. So we crossed the Bugesera, which I did not know. It was the first region which was slightly safe, because the genocide there had been interrupted. It looked like a great desert. We still could not go off into the surrounding areas though, and passengers who strayed, for instance, from the main road to look for food in the fields, had to be accompanied, for fear of marauding *interahamwe*.

When we arrived in Nyamata, we could go no further; we were dropped off at the town hall. We went looking for a roof over our heads, one or two families per room. Before the war, it was said of Nyamata that it was a good little town. But from the first glance, I saw that there had been too much war here, too many burned houses, too many scars and disabilities upon the people. The town was worse than contaminated. Above all, there were not many people left. On the road, I was told about the massacres in the churches, I knew that nearly all the inhabitants had disappeared, as in Butare. My immediate impression was that future here would be very impoverished.

Very quickly, we also saw in detail how the lives of those who remained had been overturned: no one was prepared to seek out their own way forward. We guessed that people no longer cared for anything, they could glimpse no future, there was no hope anywhere, it was as though their minds were very crippled. I will give you an example. By chance, we walked into a damaged home to pay a visit of friendship; inside we saw a little family on the ground. We said to the man: "You, why are you sleeping like this, in the dust and mess, not paying attention to your own?" Without even getting up, he answered: "I no longer care. I had a wife, she is dead. I had a house, it is crushed. I had children, several were killed. Everything that mattered to me I have lost."

As for me, I had travelled with my husband, my two children, little brothers and sisters and a newborn brought into the world during the genocide. The first three months in Nyamata, I stayed at home, hardly ever going out, taken up with household chores. Life was very difficult because there was nothing. You could spend four or five hours and still not find a full bucket of drinking water; the same for food, the same for wood.

It was not a problem not knowing anyone in the region,

because we had come in a little group from Butare, and in any case because no one seemed to recognize anybody here. Later on, in the month of September, I heard that a Canadian organization was looking for a social worker, I turned up for the interview, I landed the job. I started to travel around the hills. Then I looked into the quick of life.

At that time, rare were the vehicles driving around the town. One of them would drop us off in the bush in the morning at eight, we would set off on foot, and it would come back to pick us up in the same place at five in the afternoon. So we began walking, on a search for non-accompanied children – children without parents or adults by their side – who the killings had scattered in the hills. It still goes on today. We continue to visit homes, enter the banana groves, identifying children who have come together or who sometimes live alone in huts, without even a seat or a blanket.

Meeting such children touches me greatly, because from all sides their situation is miserable. All have escaped different stories; those who survived in the sorghum fields, those who survived in the marshes or at the bottom of a ditch, those who have travelled far, beyond their land, on hazardous roads. These children are disturbed, but not in the same way. There are those who want to speak but whose ideas are not well enough formed. Those who quite simply cannot manage to express anything but tears. Those who say: "I cried, but they still killed my papa, my maman. I cried but I have nothing to eat, I have no roof above my head. I cried but I have nothing to go to school with, now I do not even want to cry anymore, not for me, not for anyone."

There are some children who spoke very freely after the genocide, but who now are silent. They cannot see any reason to talk anymore. In the beginning, they talked about the killings as of extraordinary and terrible stories, as though they were of enormous importance, but which they thought would end in the telling, or which would end well if only they were listened

to carefully. Later, their hopes flew away with their words. Time made them understand how their lives have changed, how much these stories are true. They brood over what they lived through in the marshes, they understand that no one can replace what they have lost, they wall themselves up in a silent nightmare. There are those who are very frustrated, very confused, or very rebellious. Little by little, I got used to them.

To spin out a thread to a person who has been wounded, you must encourage him first to open up a little and unburden himself of a few thoughts, in which the knots of his disarray will appear. For this, I adopt a simple strategy. I approach this person, I am silent for a moment. I begin talking to him and say: "I too am a survivor. To me too, they did everything so I would no longer be alive. I too know that my parents are dead, a few metres in front of me I saw the *interahamwe* run people through with their spears. I too lived through this situation. As of now, the two of us are going to live with these truths." So the person begins to see me as less strange and becomes reconciled a little with trust.

The genocide is like no other torment. This is a certainty I gleaned from one hill to the next. To share the genocide in words with someone who has lived it is very different to sharing it with someone who has only heard about it elsewhere. In the genocide's wake, there persists, buried in the survivor's mind, a wound that can never show itself in broad daylight to other people. As for us, we do not know exactly what the nature of this hidden wound is, but at least we know it exists. Those who have not lived the genocide see nothing. If they try hard, then one day they will be able to acknowledge the secret pain we feel. But it will take a long time, even if these people are Tutsis from Rwanda or Burundi, even if they lost families and close relations during the killings. I cannot explain why, but I know it will be very slow. I do not know the history of other genocides; but I can guess that this delay is everywhere the same: those who have not been through a genocide, even with great effort they will through time understand a mere fraction.

The important thing with a child who has come out of a genocide is also to immediately relieve him of one aspect of his material hardship. To find him medicine if he suffers from a sickness, to open up a room for him in a house, to give him food to eat, something to wear, school things if he can go back to school, tools if he is going to farm. In this way, he sees himself as less abandoned, he knows he is more valued and he feels better in society. Next is to push him towards other children. Children talk easily amongst themselves of what they have experienced, and this frees up language. Afterwards, you much listen to each word he utters to help him unravel his problem and find new words to express himself more deeply.

There is something important I must point out: the genocide changed the meaning of certain words in the survivor's language; and it completely lifted the meaning out of other words, and so the person listening must be alert to such changes in meaning.

Nevertheless, I have noticed over time that the very youngest are not the most vulnerable after a genocide, because when these very young children begin to taste of life again, they find their former selves in a more spontaneous way. Their pleasure is still vivacious. Except of course when they are very seriously traumatized and do not speak anymore, naturally. The most difficult ages are adolescence and old age. Adolescents suffer more than others from not understanding. They cannot admit that the *interahamwe* wanted to put an end to them, without any prior threat or argument. Without a care, adolescents arrived at the doors of life and machete blows stopped them from entering. They have been in the why of it ever since. They ask: "What does my face bear that I do not know of? What do I carry on me that Hutus cannot stand, since I did nothing to them? Why did they have to massacre my parents who farmed peacefully? How shall I live near people who think only of killing me without explanation?" For many of them, adult life becomes too confused. For all these young girls, for instance, who now find themselves pregnant any old how, without forethought, without surprise, without worrying an instant as to what will happen to the baby.

That said, when adolescents come together, when they talk about this amongst themselves, they exchange answers, they share their feelings and this relieves them of their worries. There are even some who have started to speak with young Hutus, and these conversations reveal a glimmer of hope.

As for old people, they are inconsolable about what they have lost. They raised children who gave them clothes, food and tenderness for their old age and now they are left with no one around them. In killing their children, it's as if they chopped off their arms and legs at the starting line of this final stage of their life. Old people keep saying: "I fed healthy sons and daughters, I suitably married them and they died in the marshes. Who can I lean on now as I go through old age? Who can help me avoid sickness and sorrow?" They notice that from now on their sole companions are solitude and misery; it's very difficult for them not to drown their thoughts in the abyss of memory.

There are also Hutu children who walked to the Congo and who have returned home. The difference is barely visible to the eye. Except that children of this long journey can never stay put, they tend to drop school and family abruptly, they like to vanish into the thicket. When you talk to them, when you ask them how they left, with whom they travelled, what time imposed on them in the camps, how they live now, they talk a little, they let some details slip, but up comes one word and, hey presto, they escape and say they do not want any more of this conversation.

The children who survived the Nyamwiza marshes looked into evil at its darkest, for a limited period though. If you can get hold of them and gently haul them in, then it all comes out more easily.

Children who went to the Congo, however, lived in confusion and danger for a very long time. In the camps at Goma, they had to get by on their own to live, no one looked after them anymore, they saw themselves as no longer wanted by anyone, they came back like nobodies to nothing. They are not themselves anymore.

Those who came through the genocide will never get rid of what they lived through, but they can pick up the trail back to real life because they can tell the truth now, and they are surrounded by people who tell the truth. Many dangers they may be afraid of, but not those of lies.

The children who came back from the Congo still live in silence, they do not look the person they are chatting to in the eye. There are some whose parents died or disappeared during their flight. These children say they know nothing. There are some whose parents are in prison; we ask them if they know why, they are evasive. They answer that they were sick, that they were away, that they looked at nothing, heard nothing during the period of the genocide. They are always frightened that because of one misplaced word we will come looking for them too. And even if they dare say something, even if they wish to lighten their burden, if they try to reveal what they know, they do not tell the truth. They make up alibis to prove that they witnessed nothing. They fear being mistreated. And I notice without being mistaken that with the passing years they feel more and more guilty about the bad deeds of their parents.

The problems of Tutsi children who survived the killings evolve over time. Their memories are all too heavy burdens which nevertheless lighten as they are changed by time.

For Hutu children who travelled to the Congo, however, the weight remains because they cannot face the past. Silence paralyses them in fear. Time pushes them away. From one visit to the next, nothing changes. You notice that worries are permanently chasing ideas in their heads. It is difficult persuading them to speak. Still, if they say nothing of the turmoil inside them, they will never get back their hold on life. So you have to be very gentle and patient in their presence, you have to visit them very regularly, to entrust to time the budding of friendship. In some of the families I have visited since the beginning, the children have told of what happened during the genocide, what they saw with their own eyes about the house all that time, the evil their parents did. Now they are more comfortable with the children of survivors they begin to meet.

Often the children stumble over a trough of grief, or of panic, especially during sleep. In dreams they reproduce what they lived through, they shout, they cry, they sometimes start running out into the darkness or ask forgiveness. This disturbs the other children in the house and, unable to sleep, everyone waits for morning to come. If a child or an adolescent is lost in an attack of this sort, you must sit beside him and ask if he wants to talk it over. If I am there, I start talking, then he will talk to me, I tell him of everything that happened to me, and he then tells me about everything that happened to him, as I have already outlined for you, and calm comes in through the back door. I put aside some bits of my own life, but I am ready for questions. Too bad if I cannot explain to him why it happened – the main thing always is that he feels less alone for being a survivor.

I like to speak of all this with children, with acquaintances and colleagues. In any case, not a day that goes by that I do not think of these episodes; so it is beneficial to talk of them. A genocide is a film which unfolds every day before the eyes of he who came through it and it is pointless interrupting it until the end. I like my job, it does not tire me out – on the contrary. I do my work thoroughly. Talking to children helps me grow in my understanding of the genocide.

I keep my smallest children apart from it, because the moment to speak has not come. If I told them about the bad situation I escaped, my words might convey a grief, a hatred, and a frustration that little children would not be able to unravel. I risk revealing attitudes which could drive us apart.

It is a great effort to accept this, but children, if they have not lived through the killings, should not have to be subjected to their parents' troubles. Even if life has stopped for one person, it goes on for the children. When my children grow up, I will answer the questions that they will bring back from school. I will hide nothing from them, because the genocide is now engraved in Rwanda's history, but I want life to stretch out a good while for them before this blood appears.

I was born in the commune of Butare. My father was a librarian at the national university of Rwanda, my mother was a teacher in primary school. We were nine children, I was the second. We were altogether more than two hundred people in the family, living in a row of a dozen houses in a street in Runyinya, a neighbourhood eighteen kilometres from the city. I grew up in a beautiful family. I was very much looked after by grandfathers, grandmothers and those you call uncles and aunts. I never heard my parents squabbling. They earned a little money, we bought hardly anything thanks to the plot we farmed. I was very happy because I never encountered any problems. I studied Humanities, I undertook a training in social sciences, my goal was to study in university. I married a teacher with a good future who lived in a medium-sized house with a little garden I helped tend. Truly, life was good.

In Butare, Tutsis and Hutus lived mixed together without problems, above all in the teachers' neighbourhoods. There was a little *cabaret* near our home, where from way back we swapped talk and brochettes of friendship. All this changed in an instant. On the day of Habyarimana's death, a colleague who had shared beer and news with us the day before all of a sudden did not want to meet our gaze. That day, I realised the extent to which our friends looked down upon us without our having had the slightest suspicion.

In Tutsi families, we avoided talking about this war waged by soldiers from Uganda against Habyarimana's soldiers. Perhaps

Hutus talked a lot about it amongst themselves: perhaps they had nurtured a hatred for us which they kept hidden. Truly, the surprise of it stopped me from understanding anything.

So after the plane fell we were ordered to stay in our homes, without even being able to go out to the market. The soldiers guarded us, we did not know what they were up to, but we hadn't yet been killed. Around about the 9th or 10th of April, the situation became serious throughout the country. We heard, on the radio or on the grapevine, that things were going really badly in Kigali, and very bad news detailed the numbers of corpses strewn all along the roads. Where we were, however, calm persisted, except that many people began starving to death in their own houses. While waiting, we discussed it and asked ourselves questions like: since we do not know whether the plane crash was an accident, why are Hutu peasants walking in orderly file at the crack of dawn to kill Tutsi peasants? And other such words which were no more meaningful.

One morning, the soldiers opened the door and let us out to buy food for one day. It was April 19th. So my husband went to the market. When he came back, he explained to me: "It is very serious in town, the *interahamwe* have started to kill. We have to leave right now." I was very ill, I had no more strength left because of the baby, but without protest I answered: "Alright, I will go and pack a case." He said: "No, we have no time, we are leaving immediately." I put our diplomas in a small bag with clothes for the children and we left, all dishevelled-looking, the two children in our arms. By chance, we found room in a van, the cost shared with a second family. The van was making for Burundi because Butare was not far from the border.

So on the road I discovered the ferocity of war. Meaning corpses everywhere, the dying, their bodies completely opened up, stirring and moaning still, Hutus joyful with wickedness. At the customs post near the border, we were stopped at a last barrier. An immense crowd of fugitives joined us little by little: they were coming down from the hills, surging out of the rivers, they were running along the road, they were screaming. The *interahamwe* and soldiers chopped them to pieces left right and centre. Truly, these criminals were like hordes, leaving the dead and dying in their wake.

So we sat down on the ground and we waited for death. I had sloughed off my fear. I had got used to the din of screaming, I was waiting for the steel. Sometimes, you are afraid when a situation builds, but in the midst of it you keep going in a sort of anaesthetized state. I had become patient. Suddenly we heard a little burst of panicky gunfire. There was a sort of row going on amongst the soldiers, I think. I felt the baby in my belly, I thought of those future mamans gutted by machetes. I grabbed one of the children by the hand, my husband lifted the second one up onto his back, and without thinking about anything anymore I ran away from the insanity of the carnage and flung myself into the arms of a Burundian customs official. He pronounced words to the following effect. "Alright, for you, Madame, it's all over. Now you must rest." A moment later I saw a great crowd lying dead that on the other side of the road block.

I liked Butare very much. Firstly, because it was the commune I was born in, secondly because I was used to it. It was a medium-sized town where I knew many different people. Afterwards, I went back to the house where my parents were killed, to bury them like Christians. I did not stay longer than the short time necessary.

Before the war, a Rwandan could not live just anywhere, unlike in your country. He would claim: "I cannot live there where there is not my family, my house, my neighbours, my cows." If he went travelling, he would always return there where his family was born. When I visit Butare now, I feel pain, because there is no life there for me. If you can find no one to chat to in the place where you lived, you are sad. There is no longer anyone left. In the town centre, I come across a great number of new faces and I meet no one I used to know. In Butare, many faculties, university institutes and schools of higher education have all to their honour reopened since the war, nevertheless I find that intellectual life here is destroyed. I have not found more than four pupils with whom I did my studies, the others are dead. In our neighbourhood of Runyinya, only the bush has returned to occupy the ruins of our houses. We had a large family of about two hundred people, now there are only twenty of us left.

In Butare, if I meet a Hutu acquaintance, he will avoid me. He will greet me, we will ask for each other's news, then he will venture one step to the side, and he will not want us to get down to talking. Shame will immediately come between us, even should I show no rancour towards him and even if he is a good person. He will say: "Sorry, Sylvie, I have a very tight schedule" or suchlike as he rushes off.

In Rwandan custom, the neighbour is a person of very great importance. He alone knows how you woke up this morning, what it is you are missing, how he may advise you, how you may help each other. If you do not know your neighbour anymore, or if he slips away when you speak to him, something is terribly lacking and you must leave. I cannot imagine a future in Butare anymore, because the desire, neither for anything nor anybody, no longer waits for me there.

So after the genocide, it was all the same where you lived; so you settled wherever life had put you down. As for me, now, I am able to integrate to any society, if I can find a job and a roof. In Nyamata, no one is where he ought to be anymore. There are survivors from the region who cannot regain the niche they had carved out for themselves, former Tutsi exiles from Burundi and Uganda, Hutu refugees from the Congo who feel out of place. There is also great poverty in minds and in dwellings. To those sorry for themselves, I say: after a genocide, he who has still the luck to live must make the most of it without complaining.

I feel that if something good ever comes my way again, it will be in Nyamata, because this is where I found myself again. In Nyamata, I travel through the hills, I talk to many people of what is buried within their hearts. I like visiting people, talking. I like to be beside my children, to prepare a meal for them, to mend clothes, that's all.

If I do not visit foreign countries, if I cannot buy the pretty dress I spotted in a shop window in Kigali, if I am not invited to a wedding party, it does not bother me as it once did. I am no longer envious about what I do not have. I feel no need nor desire to do things in a rush, with the excuse that I nearly died and that I might not have been here to do them. I haven't even begun scratching in the little neighbourhood garden as I once did in Butare.

No, the war has not damaged my tranquillity. I am amazingly lucky, because there are other people who did more than was humanly possible to escape the machetes and who were nevertheless killed. Whereas I still live. If I have had this luck, then pleasure must waft me along at an easy tempo that suits me, neither too slow nor excessive. I see time going at its pace, I do not run after it, although I do not let it slip away without having my word to say.

Many people spend their days without doing anything, not wishing to look for work, not wanting to build walls; they are overwhelmed. They are crushed by all the mourning, they are smothered beneath misfortunes, they no longer try to look to see how they might free themselves.

There are those who want to believe life came to a standstill after the genocide, so as not to have to take stock of themselves. They keep repeating – "Why wasn't I able to save my maman? Why wasn't I able to save my child?" They are disgusted with themselves for still being here, alive, all alone. They say: "The family was all together, the killers made noise, we escaped; when we came back Maman and the children were chopped to bloody pieces." There are many people who feel guilty for being alive, or who think that by a fluke they took the place of a worthy person, or who simply feel that they are no longer of any use.

I too left many acquaintances behind me, very close ones. I am sometimes stricken by grief, but never remorse. My parents died on the 8th of April, and I didn't even hear of it at the time because I could not open my front door. The day we escaped, I watched many people dying in our wake. And I am alive, and I do not blame myself.

It happened, it should not have happened, but it happened nevertheless. I feel pain because of departed acquaintances. But even if they were cut down by axes, even if they had a very bad death, they had anyway to die that day without me. What should I have done? Should I have gone mad? Should I have stayed behind to die with them? No. I tell myself that life ended for them but it endures for me. I will simply think of them, of us, with sadness, all my life.

There were many dead around me; but I do not want to be disappointed by life, because there are also many living. I do not like these refuges where you may complain and let go of yourself. It is a weakness similar to leaving Rwanda for fear of massacres and to sit down all day saying: "If I make bricks for a home, they will demolish it, if I sew a beautiful garment, they will rip it up…" expecting nothing good will happen, neither from yourself nor from others, all huddled up beneath your black cloud.

Of course, I too often felt very humiliated on many occasions. I was living in a very talented family and it was decimated; a beautiful destiny chose me and then dropped me; I had a plan to study in university and I abandoned it. I was a fugitive, a refugee, almost a beggar, I waited to be given meagre food handouts, I lived in filth and pity. But now all this has been left to the side. If life is to go on, then it absolutely must go on! When health is not good, when tasks seem all too cumbersome, when disappointments rise up here and there about the house, it doesn't matter; every morning, I catch whatever good mood comes my way.

Deep down inside me, nothing important has changed. My life was diverted, the people in the neighbourhood are no longer the same, my work is not that which I studied for, but I still want to be the same person. I do not seek within the genocide excuses for giving up, for excusing myself. I do not know if you can understand.

In Butare, I remember the French soldiers, sweating in their new jogging suits early in the morning. On the first days of the genocide, they took off, driving all the Whites before them. What were they doing here, if they could not handle their guns? Why did they do a runner, if they knew nothing? I do not know why, but I know that the Whites never wanted to open both eyes to see the genocide.

Television cameramen and journalists came and travelled around. They watched but all they saw were extraordinary events, if I can put it like this. They saw columns of Hutus moving on the roads to the Congo and they commented: "Look at them, here are victims of war escaping death." They saw the army of RPF marching and they explained: "These are Tutsi soldiers winning the ethnic war and chasing Hutus out." But as for the people who had hidden in the marsh sludge, in ceilings, at the bottom of well holes, not even able to move an inch for weeks – no one was worried about them. On the television screens, the reporters said: "Those who have not been killed are the people now fleeing on the long roads to the camps," and in the end they completely forgot the survivors of the Tutsi massacres.

So the survivors, who could they talk to? To no one. They were caught between those who were coming and those who were leaving, and this pushed them even more to the wayside. This was barbarous for us. This dryness of the soul seemed pitiless. For weeks we had survived the machetes, we had gone through the worst without anyone reaching out a hand, and already we were no longer part of the picture. Even now, years later, things have not changed that much. There are still truths about the survivors which are hidden or incorrectly described, which prevent foreigners from acknowledging the genocide without suspicion. I mean, from being alarmed by it.

Here's a thought: the Whites who looked calmly on during the genocide now feel embarrassed about their passivity, about their deceit, so they prefer to put all the killings in the same bag, lump all wars and countries together, avoid the simple truth, and, in doing so, do not have to meet with too many survivors. So the survivors also lose respect for the truth and they say to themselves: Alright, since other people have come to arrangements with the truth, what is the point in our concerning ourselves with others?

Another important observation is that it is difficult for a White to understand certain African attitudes. Let me present a situation very common amongst us. I have a good neighbour, we appear to be on good terms, we are calm. Then one day, he bristles, he reproaches me for something without saying what it is. However, he broods over it and his gaze hardens. If I spot his evil eye in time, I will contact a friend and explain to him that something between us is going badly. This friend will go to the neighbour and talk to him. And perhaps he will come back to me and tell me: "Your neighbour is mad at you for such and such a reason, take the necessary precautions." Then I will either get up and talk things out with him, or I will keep my distance. Otherwise, a very serious row could erupt. If he bottles up bad feeling, an African can explode with a sudden violence beyond his control. This African character trait is at the root of some very unexpected killings. When they occur, Whites observe us and say, "Well, the Congolese, the Sierra-Leonians, the Angolans are killing each other again; it will blow over in the end."

In Rwanda nevertheless, Whites could not but have understood after a few days that these were not the usual massacres, but a genocide, and they did not act. This is why they will leave a stain on the survivors to conceal their contempt.

When I discuss the genocide with acquaintances to try to understand it, we put forward three ideas. The first has to do with the material conditions of life and poverty. The second idea concerns ignorance. The third has to do with influential people and the great number of people they influenced. Eight out of ten Rwandans do not know how to read; it was easy therefore to get them to accept bad thoughts that served their material interests. Before the war, I did not notice any appreciable difference between Tutsis and Hutus, because we mixed with each other, drank together and helped each other. In just one day, they took out their blades, already shining. They must certainly have concealed within a hatred which they did not manage to properly come to terms with. But this is not an explanation which accounts for the extermination.

Since then, I have sought clues which I haven't managed to uncover. I know Hutus do not feel comfortable in front of Tutsis. They have decided to no longer see them anywhere, so as to feel at ease amongst themselves. But why? I cannot answer. I do not know if on my face or my body I bear distinctive marks they cannot stand. Sometimes I say, no, it cannot be that we are slender, refined, of gentle features, all these silly things. Sometimes, I say yes, it is nevertheless these ideas which germinated among them. It's a madness so extreme that even those who killed can no longer give it credence. And those they were supposed to kill even less.

In the hills, I sometimes chat to families who took part in the killing. They say they regret what they did, what their men did. They explain: "We were told: 'Kill Tutsis and you shall have houses, you shall have plots.' But we do not really know how this could have happened." I do not understand them when they speak to me this way, but I can still listen to them. Deep down inside me, there is no question of forgiving and forgetting, only reconciliation. And there is no forgiving the White who let the killers do their work. There is no forgiving the Hutu who massacred. There can be no forgiving he who watched as his neighbour opened girls' bellies and killed the baby inside before their very eyes. It is useless wasting words talking to him about it. Only justice can forgive. First, we must think of justice for the survivors, justice which offers room for the truth, which lets fear wash away; justice so that we can be reconciled.

I remain hopeful about the future, because relations on the hills are changing, people are shyly rubbing shoulders with one another. Perhaps one day cohabitation and mutual aid will start again between families of those who were killed and those who killed. But for us it is too late, because there is something missing now. We had already taken steps in our lives, we were chopped, we retreated. It is very serious for a human being to find himself far from the place in life where once he had been.

So far, I have never met anyone who tells me he is proud to be a survivor. I have never come across anyone who has said to me: "Life is beautiful, and it has never seemed so beautiful as since the massacres when I so was scared of dying"; or like, for instance, a person who has escaped a terrible illness. Even if the survivors have found a good life, if they have a job, beautiful children, beer, their lives were still cut down.

I do not know one survivor who says he feels completely safe, that he is never afraid. There are those who are afraid of the hills and who must farm nevertheless. There are those who are afraid of meeting Hutus on the road. There are Hutus who saved Tutsis, but who do not dare come to their villages, fearing that they will not be believed. There are people who are afraid of visits and of the night. There are the faces of the innocent which inspire fear, and who fear they inspire fear like the faces of criminals. There is the fear of danger, the panic about memories.

I will give you an example. Last week, we went in the van into the bush to identify children in a new area. We lost the track for all the leaves. I said to the driver: "Alright, we have got lost, but still we can keep going until we have finished today's tasks." At the edge of a banana grove we encountered a gathering of Hutu peasants at work. They stopped chopping the branches, they looked at us without saying a word, arms still. I heard myself shouting: "That's it, this time we are done for, we are all going to die." I was more than frightened, I did not know where I was anymore, my eyes could see nothing clearly, I believed we were in a real nightmare. I was crying, I kept saying to the driver: "Can't you see them, all these men with their machetes?" He put his hand on my arm, he said to me: "No, Sylvie, it's normal, it's farmers doing some pruning in their grove." He tried hard to calm me down. It was first time since I began travelling into the bush that it took hold of me again, I was so frightened that day!

I often regret the time wasted thinking of this evil. I say to myself that this fear eats into the time luck has set aside for us. I keep trying to joke with myself: "Alright, if someone wants to chop me again, let him go and get his machete – I am after all only a surviving person, let him kill whoever must be killed", and I amuse myself with this fantasy.

Because if you dwell too long in fear of genocide, you lose hope. You lose what you have managed to salvage of life. You run the risk of being contaminated by another madness. When, in calm moments, I think about the genocide I think about it so as to know where to put it in my life, but I can find no place. I simply mean that it is beyond the human.

Written in Nyamata in April, 2000

Glossary

Boyeste: Feminine equivalent of boy; a young domestic.

Foufou: A glutinous, baked dough made from manioc. In Nyamata, Edith, who loves it too, makes the best.

RPF: The Rwandan Patriotic Front. A Tutsi movement, it was founded in 1988 in the Ugandan maquis. The RPF began military operations in 1990, launched a vast offensive on first day of the genocide and finally seized control of the country on 4th July, 1994, under the command of Paul Kagame.

Gonolek: Bird whose song is of an incredible resonance. Jade black on top, scarlet plumage beneath. The crown of the head is yellow.

Inkotanyi: Meaning "invincible". Name given to RPF rebels, the Rwandan Patriotic Front.

Interahamwe: Meaning "unity". Name for extremist Hutu militia, created by the party of President Juvénal Habyarimana. They were trained by the Rwandan army; and in certain localities by French soldiers. They were armed mainly with machetes and other weapons with blades provided by the army, the administration and notables. These militia, which consisted of tens of thousands of activists, enlisted and supported the genocide's killers.

Mwami: Tutsi king.

Primus: Of Belgian origin, it is the most popular brand of beer. It is brewed in Gisenyi, in the west of Rwanda, and is sold in litre bottles only. Cheap, very slightly bitter, with a standard alcoholic content, it is usually drunk lukewarm. It divides the world of Rwandan drinkers into two opposing camps. Its fans cannot tolerate the idea of one day having to drink a single mouthful of its rival Mutzig, brewed in Burundi, or the insipid Amstel.

Talapoin: A small acrobatic monkey which lives in groups of ten and upwards, and which romp about in the water.

Tomako, touraco, soui-manga, jaco: Some of the many magical birds that live in the hills.

Umuniyinya: A huge tree, called a chit-chat tree because of its height and the size of its shade-giving leaves.

Umunzenze: Huge tree of the marshes.

Urwagwa: Banana wine, very cheap, more or less strong and bitter, to be drunk in the three days after fermentation.

Note: At birth, each Rwandan baby is given a Rwandan name and, at the age of baptism, a western Christian name. The Rwandan names of killers mentioned in these accounts have been removed from the text, because the majority of these people are still at large or are awaiting trial.

The photographs in this book were taken by Raymond Depardon, member of the Magnum agency, regular visitor and friend to Africa, during a stay in Nyamata from 1st to the 15th August, 1999, on the author's request (except for the photograph on page 89, which is by the author himself).

Survivors Fund (SURF) is a charity dedicated to aiding and assisting the survivors of the Rwandan genocide. Since 1997, SURF has been supporting medical care for women survivors with HIV/AIDS, providing counselling for survivors, vocational training and home building for orphans. These are just some of the projects that SURF funds to help survivors rebuild a sense of self and trust in humanity. Programmes are delivered through partner organisations, including AVEGA and Uyisenga N' Manzi in Rwanda, and Bene Ubumwe in the UK.

Founded by Mary Kayitesi-Blewitt at the behest of survivors, after herself losing 50 family members during the genocide, the charity is supported by, amongst others, the Department for International Development, Comic Relief, Elton John AIDS Foundation, and Diana, Princess of Wales Memorial Fund.

Individual donations are vital to help SURF continue to make a vital difference to the lives of survivors in Rwanda and the UK. To contribute, volunteer or learn more, please visit www.survivors-fund.org.uk, call +44 (0)20 7610 2589 or write to:

Survivors Fund
10 Rickett Street
London SW6 1RU
UK

Survivors Fund (SURF) is a registered charity number 1065705.